I0541962

GIRL,
GET YOUR LIFE BACK

Nellie Griffith

Along with Contributing Authors,

Cynthia Young, Angela Papoutsakis,
Shawnnett Gaines, Lori Vober,
and Michelle Herndon McKay

© Bringing your words to life

Copyright © 2023 Trinity Publishing Company

ISBN: **979-8-9881665-4-2**

All rights reserved. This book or any portion thereof may not be reproduced or used in any manner whatsoever without the author's express written permission except for the use of brief quotations in a book review. This book may not be copied or reprinted for commercial gain or profit. The use of quotations or occasional page copying for personal, or group study is permitted.

For permission requests, write the author at the email address: **ggylb2022 @gmail.com**

Cover Design: Nellie A. Griffith

Editing: Dorcas Kate

Formatting: Paul Nomshan

Dedication

First giving all Honor, All Glory and All Praise to my LORD and Savior, JESUS CHRIST. It is through HIM, I live, move and have my very being.

I dedicate this book to the two greatest women of my life:

My fellow Stroke Survivor, my grandmother, Nellie Hart Oliver, the strongest woman I've ever known. The longer I live I find I'm truly a chip off the old block. I love you forever Big Nellie.

My greatest supporter, my mother, Dorothy Oliver Griffith. Without her I would never have made it this far. Thanks for Everything Mom. I love you.

Acknowledgments

First, I give all honor, glory, and praise to my LORD, JESUS CHRIST. HE's my Way Maker and my Miracle Worker. I could not have made it through the stroke, the recovery, and beyond if it was not for HIM.

To my mother, Dorothy, there is nothing like a mother's love and I want her to know how much I love and appreciate her all the time. We've been through some things but we went through them together. There's nothing I wouldn't do for you. I love you, Mom!

To my brother, Rupert, and my aunt Maria, and the family near and far for their prayers.

To my personal friends, Facebook friends, church friends, childhood friends, and my brothers and sisters in Christ who know the worth of prayer, I thank you!

To the five ladies of "Girl, Get Your Life Back", thank you for your bravery and selflessness to share your unique journey of hope and encouragement with all those who are in that place of depression, sadness, hopelessness, and anxiety.

Contents

Introduction

"Girl, Get Your Life Back," an anthology of true stories from six ladies who were going about their day-to-day lives and suffered a stroke or endured some type of brain injury. These ladies had to be resilient and fight through their own pain and struggles with what comes with brain injuries. Each person's story is different and they tell you about life before the stroke, the effects of it, and their way back to living life in abundance.

STROKE is a very serious condition that many people don't understand, take lightly, and don't respect. It's important to learn what stroke is, its causes, and warning signs so that if it happens to someone you know and/or love, you can be prepared.

I hope you read and take in this information with the understanding that no 2 strokes, no 2 recoveries, and no 2 results are the same. The Centers for Disease Control has stated

- Stroke is the No. 5 cause of death and a leading cause of disability in the United States
- Stroke kills more than 137,000 people a year. That's about 1 of every 18 deaths.
- Every 40 seconds, someone in the United States has a stroke. Every 3 minutes and 14 seconds, someone dies of a stroke.
- Every year, more than **795,000** people in the United States have a stroke. About 610,000 of these are first or new strokes.
- About 185,000 strokes – **nearly 1 in 4** –are in people who have had a previous stroke.
- About **87%** of all strokes are ischemic strokes, in which blood flow to the brain is blocked.

What Is Stroke?

A stroke or brain attack happens when blood flow to the brain is blocked by a clot or bursts (or ruptures). This prevents the brain from getting oxygen and nutrients from the blood. If the blood supply is stopped even for a short time, this can cause problems. Brain cells begin to die after just a few minutes without blood or oxygen.

When brain cells die, they generally do not regenerate and devastating damage may occur, sometimes resulting in physical, cognitive, and mental disabilities. You may not be able to do things that are controlled by that part of the brain. For example, a stroke may affect your ability to:

- Move
- Speak
- Eat
- Think and remember
- Control your bowel and bladder
- Control your emotions
- Control other vital body functions

A stroke can happen to anyone at any time. It is the No. 5 cause of death and a leading cause of disability in the United States.

A stroke is a medical emergency. A stroke can cause lasting brain damage, long-term disability, or even death every minute counts.

Types of Strokes

There are typically 3 types of Stroke but the American Stroke Association has identified 5 types.

1. **Ischemic Stroke** occurs when a vessel supplying blood to the brain is obstructed. It accounts for about 87 % of all strokes

   a. *Thrombotic (cerebral thrombosis)* is the most common type of ischemic stroke. A blood clot forms inside a diseased or damaged artery in the brain resulting from atherosclerosis (cholesterol-containing deposits called plaque), blocking blood flow.

   b. *Embolic (cerebral embolism)* is a blood clot that forms at another location in the circulatory system, usually the heart and large arteries of the upper chest and neck. Part of the blood clot breaks loose enters the bloodstream, and travels through the brain's blood vessels until it reaches vessels too small to let it pass. A main cause of embolism is an irregular heartbeat called atrial fibrillation. It can cause clots to form in the heart, dislodge and travel to the brain.

2. **Hemorrhagic strokes** make up about 13 % of stroke cases. They're caused by a weakened vessel that ruptures and bleeds into the surrounding brain. The blood accumulates and compresses the surrounding brain tissue.

A hemorrhagic stroke occurs when a weakened blood vessel ruptures. Two types of weakened blood vessels usually cause hemorrhagic stroke:

- Aneurysms – An aneurysm is a weak area in a blood vessel that usually enlarges. It's often described as a "ballooning" of the blood vessel. Most develop after age 40. Aneurysms usually develop at branching points of arteries and are caused by constant pressure from blood flow. They often enlarge slowly and become weaker as they grow, just as a balloon becomes weaker as it stretches.
- Arteriovenous (AVMs) - Normally, arteries carry blood containing oxygen from the heart to the brain, and veins carry blood with less oxygen away from the brain and back to the heart. When an arteriovenous malformation (AVM) occurs, a tangle of blood vessels in the brain bypasses normal brain tissue and directly diverts blood from the arteries to the veins. Brain AVMs occur in less than 1 % of

the population. AVMs are more common in males than in females. Brain AVMs are usually congenital, meaning someone is born with one. But they're usually not hereditary.

The two types of hemorrhagic strokes are intracerebral (within the brain) hemorrhage and subarachnoid hemorrhage:

- Intracerebral Hemorrhage - bleeding that occurs within the brain tissue. Many intracerebral hemorrhages are due to changes in the arteries caused by long-term hypertension. Other potential causes may be delineated through testing.
- Subarachnoid Hemorrhage - bleeding that occurs in the space between the surface of the brain and skull. A common cause of subarachnoid hemorrhagic stroke is a ruptured cerebral aneurysm, an area where a blood vessel in the brain weakens, resulting in a bulging or ballooning out of part of the vessel wall; or the rupture of an arteriovenous malformation (AVM), a tangle of abnormal and poorly formed blood vessels (arteries and veins), with an innate propensity to bleed.

3. Transient Ischemic Attack (TIA) is a temporary blockage of blood flow to the brain. The clot usually dissolves on its own or gets dislodged, and the symptoms usually last less than five minutes.

While a TIA doesn't cause permanent damage, it's a "warning stroke" signaling a possible full-blown stroke ahead. When you first notice symptoms, get help immediately, even if symptoms go away.

4. Cryptogenic Stroke or Stroke of Unknown Cause In most cases, a stroke is caused by a blood clot that blocks blood flow to the brain. But in some instances, despite testing, the cause can't be determined. Strokes without a known cause are called cryptogenic. It is estimated that about 1 in 3 ischemic strokes are cryptogenic

Some studies suggest that the incidence of cryptogenic stroke is higher in African-Americans (two times more likely) and Hispanics (46% more likely).

Possible Hidden Causes of Stroke

- Irregular heartbeat (atrial fibrillation) – AFib patients are at a 5 times greater risk for stroke.
- Heart structure problem (such as Patent Foramen Ovale)
- Hardening of the arteries (Large Artery Atherosclerosis)
- Blood clotting disorder (Thrombophilia)

5. Brain Stem Stroke can have complex symptoms, and they can be difficult to diagnose. A person may have vertigo, dizziness, and severe imbalance without the hallmark of most strokes — weakness on one side of the body. The symptoms of vertigo dizziness or imbalance usually occur together; dizziness alone is not a sign of stroke. A brain stem stroke can also cause double vision,

slurred speech, and decreased consciousness.

Only a half-inch in diameter, the brain stem controls all basic activities of the central nervous system: consciousness, blood pressure, and breathing. All motor control for the body flows through it. Brain stem strokes can impair any or all of these functions. More severe brain stem strokes can cause locked-in syndrome, a condition in which survivors can move only their eyes.

If a stroke in the brain stem results from a clot, the faster blood flow can be restored, the better the chances for recovery. Patients should receive treatment as soon as possible for the best recovery.

Like all strokes, brain stem strokes produce a wide spectrum of deficits and recovery. Whether a survivor has minor or severe deficits depends on the location of the stroke within the brain stem, the extent of the injury, and how quickly treatment is provided.

Recovery is possible. Because brain stem strokes do not usually affect language ability, the patient is often able to participate more fully in rehabilitation. Double vision and vertigo usually resolve after several weeks of recovery in mild to moderate brain stem strokes.

Risk Factors
of Stroke

Anyone can have a stroke at any age. But your chance of having a stroke increases if you have certain risk factors. Some risk factors for stroke can be changed or managed, while others can't.

Risk factors for stroke that can be changed, treated, or medically managed:

- **High blood pressure.** A blood pressure of 140/90 or higher can damage blood vessels (arteries) that supply blood to the brain.
- **Heart disease.** Heart disease is the second most important risk factor for stroke and the major cause of death among survivors of stroke. Heart disease and stroke have many of the same risk factors.
- **Diabetes.** People with diabetes are at greater risk

for a stroke than someone without diabetes.

- **Smoking.** Smoking almost doubles your risk for an ischemic stroke.
- **Birth control pills (oral contraceptives)**
- **History of TIAs (transient ischemic attacks).** TIAs are often called mini-strokes. They have the same symptoms as stroke, but the symptoms don't last. If you have had one or more TIAs, you are almost 10 times more likely to have a stroke than someone of the same age and sex who has not had a TIA.
- **High red blood cell count.** A significant increase in the number of red blood cells thickens the blood and makes clots more likely. This raises the risk of stroke.
- **High blood cholesterol and lipids.** High cholesterol levels can contribute to thickening or hardening of the arteries (atherosclerosis) caused by a buildup of plaque. Plaque is a deposit of fatty substances, cholesterol, and calcium. Plaque buildup on the inside of the artery walls can decrease the amount of blood flow to the brain. A stroke occurs if the blood supply is cut off to the brain.
- **Lack of exercise**
- **Obesity**
- **Excessive alcohol use.** More than 2 drinks per day raise your blood pressure. Binge drinking can lead to stroke.
- **Illegal drugs.** IV (intravenous) drug abuse carries a high risk of stroke from blood clots (cerebral

embolisms). Cocaine and other drugs have been closely linked to strokes, heart attacks, and many other cardiovascular problems.

- **Abnormal heart rhythm.** Some types of heart disease can raise your risk for stroke. Having an irregular heartbeat (atrial fibrillation) is the most powerful and treatable heart risk factor for stroke.
- **Cardiac structural abnormalities.** Damaged heart valves (valvular heart disease) can cause long-term (chronic) heart damage. Over time, this can raise your risk for stroke.

Risk factors for stroke that can't be changed:

- **Older age.** For each decade of life after age 55, your chance of having a stroke more than doubles.
- **Race.** African Americans have a much higher risk for death and disability from a stroke than whites. This is partly because the African-American population has a greater incidence of high blood pressure.
- **Gender.** Stroke occurs more often in men, but more women than men die from stroke.
- **History of prior stroke.** You are at higher risk for having a second stroke after you have already had a stroke.
- **Heredity or genetics.** The chance of stroke is greater in people with a family history of stroke.

Other risk factors include:

- **Where you live.** Strokes are more common among

people living in the southeastern U.S. than in other areas. This may be because of regional differences in lifestyle, race, smoking habits, and diet.

- **Temperature, season, and climate.** Stroke deaths occur more often during extreme temperatures.
- **Social and economic factors.** There is some evidence that strokes are more common among low-income people.

Symptoms of Stroke

F.A.S.T. Warning Signs

Use the letters in F.A.S.T. to Spot a Stroke

- **F = Face Drooping** – Does one side of the face droop or is it numb? Ask the person to smile. Is the person's smile uneven?
- **A = Arm Weakness** – Is one arm weak or numb? Ask the person to raise both arms. Does one arm drift downward?
- **S = Speech Difficulty** – Is speech slurred?
- **T = Time to call 911**

Stroke is the No. 5 cause of death and a leading cause of disability in the U.S. Stroke can happen to anyone — any age, any time — and everyone needs to know the warning signs.

On average, 1.9 million brain cells die every minute that a stroke goes untreated.

Stroke is an EMERGENCY.

Call 911 immediately.

Early treatment leads to higher survival rates and lower disability rates. Calling 911 lets first responders start treatment on someone experiencing stroke symptoms before arriving at the hospital.

Other Stroke Symptoms

Watch for Sudden:

- **NUMBNESS** or weakness of face, arm, or leg, especially on one side of the body
- **CONFUSION,** trouble speaking or understanding speech
- **TROUBLE SEEING** in one or both eyes
- **TROUBLE WALKING** dizziness, loss of balance or coordination
- **SEVERE HEADACHE** with no known cause

ARE SYMPTOMS OF STROKES DIFFERENT FOR MEN AND WOMEN?

Men and women who have strokes often feel similar symptoms of stroke, such as face drooping, arm weakness, and speech difficulty.

Other common signs for both women and men include problems seeing out of one or both eyes and balance or coordination problems.

Women can also experience:

- General weakness
- Disorientation and confusion or memory problems
- Fatigue, nausea, or vomiting

However, some signs of stroke in women can be subtle enough to be missed or brushed off. That can lead to delays in getting time-sensitive, lifesaving treatments.

WHAT ARE SILENT STROKES AND DO THEY HAVE SYMPTOMS?

Silent strokes are undetected strokes. They occur when a blood vessel blockage in the brain causes cells to die, but no warning signs or symptoms are obvious.

About one-fourth of people over age 80 have at least one such area of tissue death, known as a "silent infarct," in the brain. The condition is more common with increasing age, and in people who smoke or have a history of vascular disease (conditions that affect your blood vessels).

Experts estimate that 10 silent strokes occur for every stroke with detectable symptoms. Despite being called "silent," these infarcts have been linked to subtle problems in a person's movement and mental processing. They also are linked to future risk for stroke and dementia.

Silent infarcts can be seen in patients through advanced brain imaging techniques such as MRI and CT.

All of that is REAL. A stroke happens to real-life people in many ways. Going forward, you will find the journey of 6 courageous and determined who wouldn't let Stroke take over their lives. These stories of Hope will encourage you to know that there is more life to live after a stroke.

Citations:

1. American Association of Neurological Surgeons
https://www.aans.org/Patients
Neurosurgical-Conditions-and-Treatments/Stroke

2. American Stroke Association
https://www.stroke.org

3. Centers for Disease Control and Prevention
https://www.cdc.gov/stroke/facts.htm

4. John Hopkins School of Medicine
https://www.hopkinsmedicine.org/health/
conditions-and-diseases/stroke

Nellie A. Griffith,

The Visionary of Girl, Get Your Life Back

Nellie overcame the hardship that came along with the effects of the stroke. She had the vision to gather other ladies virtually from different parts of the world, and she wrote it down and held it close to her heart as she desired to have each person tell their story. It's been nine years since her stroke and today we see what 'Write the Vision' can do. Not only are these ladies now able to tell their stories, but they have become authors. As the scripture tells us in Jeremiah 32:17, "There is nothing too hard for God!"

There Is Life After Stroke!

I can't believe this is finally here. My stroke. My story. My journey. Writing my stroke journey has helped me to process all that has happened to me before, during, and after. Along the way, I've learned so much, so many lessons that will be with me for the rest of my life. As I share, I want to drop in some of them that I hope will encourage and help others who have gone through their own stroke or traumatic experience.

Before...

"Hi, my name is Nellie and I had a stroke"

I'm not the Nellie in that statement. There was one before. Nellie Oliver, my grandmother whom we affectionately called GaGa. She was the first person I ever knew personally who was a stroke survivor. When I heard the term "stroke", I had no idea what it meant. All I knew was that something happened to her and she wasn't quite the same. There was a lot of whispering and hush-hush conversations. The family said she had high blood pressure but she had HBP for years, so she took a water pill and didn't eat salt, for years. She was in the nursing home, still talking but couldn't walk because her left side was affected. My grandmother was very strong-willed. She was there until they made the decision to take her home to my aunt's house. She had a home attendant seven days a week. My mother and aunts took care of her. They had a rotation, which included me for a while. They have no idea how this affected me. Yes, I was an adult, but this was my grandmother, my Big Nellie. I had never seen her like this. She looked so small and at times, helpless. You could tell she wanted to do things for herself but couldn't. She didn't want me to help take care of her and I didn't want to do it. I was selfish in my head for a while. Why was I the only grandchild tasked with this? This was not my responsibility. I wasn't one of the daughters. I should be able to just go see my grandmother, not "work".

Lesson:

It's not about me. It's about love

My Big Nellie would let me wash her, feed her, sing, and laugh, but adamantly didn't want me to change her. She would fight me on this. She would keep moving my hand, and wouldn't cooperate when I asked her to do something. One day, I had to tell her how much I loved her and I understood why she didn't want me to do that for her, to see her in that way but that's part of how I get to show my love for her. That day forever changed the love in my heart for her. Then she started deteriorating right before our very eyes. She stopped speaking. Her motor skills went down. She still had understanding and could mouth words but some of that spunk was gone.

Side note: My grandmother had the best attendants, especially Irma. She didn't let my grandmother just sit at home in front of a TV. She would talk with her, and take her all over New York City by bus or train. She cared for her but didn't allow her to be stuck. My grandmother loved her days out with Irma. She treated my grand-mother like her own and called her Gaga like everyone else. Big ups to all the caregivers for the job you do every day. You are appreciated.

My mother wanted a better atmosphere, a better environment for my grandmother. My mom is the eldest daughter and wanted to leave the city, move south and take my grandmother with her. To this day, I swear she did "pin-the-tail" to choose which city because we knew nothing about Raleigh, North Carolina. We didn't know anyone there and had never gone there. I couldn't let her go alone to care for my grandmother. So we went together, bought a house, moved in, and later sent for Gaga. She was excited, just smiling when she got off the plane. They said she smiled the whole time. When we got to the house, she sat on the porch with her face to the sun. I asked her how she liked it. Her eyes were so bright. I began to sing our song, "It is well with my soul". That was such a great day.

After some time, we ended up taking her to the hospital and eventually, she was placed in a nursing facility. That was hard on my mother. Mom went to see Gaga every day, twice a day. I went once a day, sometimes twice. My aunts were still in NYC but they came regularly and as often as they could. It's hard to see someone you love, even after months and years still be affected. God put some really good people, HIS people around her, and I will forever be thankful for the nurses, CNAs, and staff.

To understand my story, I had to tell some of Gaga's story. My grandmother was strong, resilient, sassy, and direct but loving, and I wouldn't be here today without her.

Lesson:

Listen when your body speaks to you

About a year before moving to North Carolina, I was diagnosed with diabetes. No one in my family ever experienced this disease that I am aware of. I didn't understand why I had it, and I didn't understand any symptoms until my eyesight started to become blurry and I experienced frequent urination. My sugar level was at 650 the first time I was tested. I was younger and thought that was an old person's disease. So now, I'm in NC, taking care of my grandmother but then she passes away. Looking back, it took so much out of me. I leaned on her so much, even more than my mother. That was MY Gaga. I'm named after her. The other grandchildren loved her, no doubt but it wasn't the same connection. Little did I know how much I would come to rely on the connection we had.

I wasn't aware that I was having symptoms of a stroke. I didn't have all the typical symptoms; numbness, trouble speaking, confusion, loss of balance, or coordination. I would have the occasional headache. I'd get light-headed at times. I honestly thought it was due to either my sugar levels or eating habits. I may have had some of those other symptoms, but I wasn't listening to my body. Not only that, even if I was listening, I was too scared to go to the doctor. The scariest thing I experienced before the stroke happened while driving on the highway. I was on the way home one afternoon like every other day. I'm not even sure how it happened but I looked up and realized I was in a whole different lane than I remembered. I realized I had blacked out. What's crazy is that didn't happen only once but at least two other times. Still, I didn't listen to my body.

My Stroke And Recovery

On the night of December 7, 2013, I went to a women's fellowship at a friend's house in Raleigh. Everything was going well. All the ladies had a great time. I drove home on the dark winding road but I made it home without any incident. I parked, went into the house, and lost all track of time. I remember my right arm feeling funny like it was half numb lengthwise. I came out of my bedroom and my brother asked me what was wrong. I told him and I remembered him saying he was going to call my childhood friend and nurse Diana. It was weird to me because Diana lives in the Bronx. I then remember her being on the phone, asking me what was wrong. I told her what I had felt but it passed. She said if it happens again go to the hospital. I went back into the room. I was like in a fog. Everything was moving in slow motion, and the numbness returned.

My mother came out and asked me my name. I answered, Nellie. She asked me her name and I responded Nellie again. She told me to get dressed, we were going to the hospital. I was wondering when/how did I get undressed!

The next thing I remember was trying to get down the stairs but I couldn't walk. My brother and mother had to carry me to the car. My mind is still in a time warp, I felt. We got to the hospital, I jumped out of the car and started walking sideways. They put me in a wheelchair and took me to the back, and that's when everything went black.

Part of what happened next is recollections of what my family told me.

The left side of my brain was severely hemorrhaging. I was in the ICU where the doctors placed me in an induced coma. I was told they wanted to operate and drain the blood from my brain. The following morning right before taking me to surgery, a nurse said to check one more time and the blood was miraculously gone but I was still in the coma. They told my mother I would not come out of the coma but if I did, I would be a vegetable for the rest of my life. BUT GOD!

I was moved to another room out of ICU. I sort of remember waking up a couple of times. I saw my brother once and at another time I saw a minister from the church but I went back out. My mom told me while I was in the coma, this older doctor came into my room. She had never seen him before. He looked at me, looked at my chart, looked at me again then told her that I was going to be fine then never saw him again.

Then one day I woke up with the need to go to the bathroom. I looked around, everything was out of focus. I didn't have my glasses on. I looked around but couldn't find them. I really had to go, so I stood up getting ready to go somewhere then realized I had an IV in my arm. I couldn't understand what was happening. I couldn't see and had to pee. A nurse walked by and stopped in. I asked her to please help me get unhooked so I could go to the bathroom. She asked what make me think I could go to the bathroom. I looked at her and told her because I could! She told me to sit and she would help me. I must have fallen asleep because when I looked up again, all the doctors, all the nurses, my mom, just everybody was in the room. They asked me basic questions (i.e., my name, age, where I lived, etc.). I remember telling them I had to go to the bathroom. They all scrambled and the nurse unhooked the IV and the catheter and helped me to the bathroom. She said they were very happy to see me awake. I was told I had been in a coma. I asked the nurse how long. She told me three days! I could have jumped out of the bed and run around. My JESUS was in the grave for three days and then HE rose! Glory to GOD!

The doctors were in and out all day. They were asking questions to test my mind. I asked for my book of Sudoku and began doing the puzzles with a pen.

Lesson:

The things you learn after will
astound and humble you

I left the hospital exactly a week after when I went in. I was happy to be home for my birthday. There was so much to process. I still didn't really understand fully what happened to me. The Neurologist said my pressure was so high, it was amazing I was still living. He told me not only did I have the stroke, but I also had two seizures. I had no idea. He then told me I couldn't drive for six months.

I attended physical therapy. When the therapist called my name, she said, "Let me shake the hand of a bonafide miracle. I read your chart and there is no way you should be walking in here unassisted and in your right mind." We both ended up in tears by the end of that session. Later, I had an appointment with the Speech Therapist and later the Occupational Therapist.

Both therapists, after the one session told me I didn't need them, however, I stayed in Physical Therapy for six weeks.

In the months following, I did a lot of praying and reading the Bible. A lot. I was totally grateful, thankful, and truly blessed. My relationship with GOD was strengthened like never before. I didn't know everything, but I did know I didn't have to still be in the land of the living. But I found myself asking GOD, Why? Why the stroke? Why me? Why did you do this to me? What did I do wrong? What should I do now? I know a lot of people don't believe you shouldn't ask GOD anything. Just take your blessing and shut up. Some people get mad at GOD because this happened to them. I believe when you have a relationship, you can ask anything. GOD already knows what going on with you. The answer that came back to me was; Why not you? You didn't do anything wrong. I had to redirect your path. I allowed this to happen and there will be glory after this.

I had some interesting things happen as a result of the stroke as well. One thing was that my taste buds changed. Anyone that knows me knows how much I love chicken. It didn't matter how you made it; fried, baked, bar-b-que, stewed, jerked, cacciatore, fricassee, curry, etc. It didn't matter. I loved it all. After the stroke, I could not eat any chicken. It was nasty to me no matter how it was cooked. I couldn't believe it myself. At the same time, I had a taste for real mashed potatoes. Not the fake, in a box but the real deal boiled and mashed potatoes. Both the chicken thing and the mashed potatoes thing went on for about eight months. Then it just changed like that. I could go back and enjoy my beloved chicken again but now my taste buds went to hot sauce. Everything had to have hot sauce and still does. My doctor said changes in my taste like that can happen due to a stroke.

Another amazing thing was that my creative mind came alive in the months following. I dug into the research of what happened to me. When I learned about the left brain vs. right brain, I wasn't surprised that I have dominant left-brain traits. Because I had a left-brain hemorrhage, during my healing time, the right side kicked in. I never considered myself a creative person. I'm logical, technical, and methodical. I found myself writing music, poetry, and dancing, and I began getting into design. Some postings on Facebook led to clients who not only liked my work but trusted me enough to pay me to learn how to design mobile apps. That really blew my mind (no pun intended).

My last appointment with the Neurologist was about five months after the stroke. He checked me out, asked a host of questions about the doctors and therapy, looked at my eyes, checked my reflexes, and asked if I was driving yet. I let him know it hadn't been six months yet. He told me I was ready. "You can drive again." I was really ecstatic because I couldn't get around besides walking. The amazing part was I found out later that most people who have had a stroke, needed to take the driving test again and I never did.

What I didn't expect because of the stroke was losing my friends. Not just any friends but my closest friends, my inner circle. That was really hard. They just stopped talking to me. We were friends for 15 to 20 years each. My feelings were deeply hurt. Someone said to me that not everyone can handle illness. Logically, I understood that but it didn't lessen the pain. I forgave but I had to let them go. Eventually, two of them contacted me again after several years.

Getting My Life Back

GOD gave me, "Girl, Get Your Life Back" in late 2014. Cute to say but what did that look like? What did that really mean? At that point, I'm still recovering, food not tasting right, still hated chicken, no income as I didn't get a disability, and didn't have a job, struggling with my diabetes numbers, abandonment, loneliness, memory loss, and still feeling sluggish, still sleeping all the time, feeling insecure in myself, my abilities. How does a girl get her life back from all of that?

Trust GOD.

I had to apologize to GOD and repent for thinking HE put this stroke on me. I had to remember GOD always had me. HE never left nor forsaken me through it all. I had to let HIM have control of my life. HE knows better than I ever could what's best for me. HE had a direction

HE wanted me to go, and I had to get on board with HIS plan. Jeremiah 29:11 reads, *"For I know the plans I have for you,"* declares the Lord, *"plans to prosper you and not to harm you, plans to give you hope and a future."*

Accept the New Me

If anyone is getting their life back after a stroke or any traumatic experience, you must Accept Your New You. It's so easy to get stuck in your head thinking, "I can't do what I used to do," or "I wish I was like I was before." I couldn't keep thinking like that and move forward. I needed a transformation of my mind concerning me. I needed to accept that I would never be the same. I've been changed forever and that's okay. I had to look at myself differently. I needed to get to know who this new Nellie was. Accept who she is, what she could do, what she couldn't do, what she didn't want to do anymore. I took a deep dive into myself. I learned to really like her. I had to start believing in myself, loving me, valuing me, learning my strengths, and accepting my weaknesses. I won't take life and living for granted. I'm more determined to live life to the fullest.

Back to School

In 2015, I was led to check out a small college in my neighborhood. I was a little hard-headed about going as I said back to GOD, "Lord, that school is expensive and I don't have any money to attend as I didn't have any income." GOD's answer to me was "I didn't ask you about your money." So I went to the school, met the Director of

Admissions, went to an open house, paid a deposit and I was back in school. I've been to college before but never graduated. I didn't want to repeat that and I didn't want to take on more than I could handle. So I enrolled in the two-year certificate program for Interactive Media Arts. I wanted to know for myself that I could complete what I started.

My experience at this school was nothing short of extraordinary!

I was one of the oldest students attending in-person classes. Here I am in my late 40s and a stroke survivor, in classes with all these 18, 19, and 20-year-olds. I was like a fish out of water. It was totally intimidating. They were already exposed to Adobe software and design techniques. All I knew was PowerPoint and MS Word. They wanted me to do things I never imagined doing. There was an instructor in my beginning year, and to this day I will forever be thankful because I would have never made it through the first class much less the rest of the year. He and I were about the same age, and he would make me feel at ease with being there by making references to things that only we were old enough to know or telling corny jokes that only we laughed at. He would assure me that I was just as good as anyone else in the class. Sometimes I felt he was just being nice, but it worked. I thanked him for helping me to believe in myself at a time when I knew I couldn't keep up.

As I continued in my classes, I really started seeing the

hand of GOD move. My purpose for being at school was not just for me and what I thought I wanted to accomplish. There were lives I had to touch. GOD made such ways for me while I was there. I started classes in the Fall of 2015, was given a job on the front desk evenings in June 2016, was asked to be a school Ambassadors and part of student government, and had my first graduation with my first certificate in Digital Media in August 2016, was offered to go into the diploma program January 2017, started teaching the Student Bible Study Group in January 2017, graduated with the Interactive Media Design Diploma August 2017, graduated with my second certificate in Internet Development in March 2018. Although I was done with school, I continued to work the front desk and teach Bible Study. In October 2018, the Vice President invited me to come back for the degree program. I told him I didn't have the finances for the courses. He said he didn't ask about that. He asked the question, "Do you want to start in January?" I started classes in January 2019, the pandemic began, started online school, and graduated with my BA in Interactive Media Arts in June 2020. They surprised me as I was named Salutatorian and gave a speech at graduation.

I was given the opportunity to complete what I never thought I could. Along the way, I met some wonderful talented students, great instructors, and staff who became part of my life for those years. I was able to pour life and wisdom into them as much as they poured into me.

Lesson:

Take the Risk: Don't be afraid of
doing something new

Entrepreneurship

I hadn't worked since right before the stroke. While
I was in school, starting my own business, was taught
and encouraged alongside getting a job in the creative
industry. I already doubted my abilities as a graphic/web
designer. My skills were okay but in comparison to
how these young people moved, I was very doubtful
about my ability to keep up with the industry trends
and these younger minds. I had a shoe and
accessories business before the stroke. My technical
mind was strong as I was always into computers. I
couldn't see myself starting a business now after the
stroke.

Lesson:

Sometimes other people can see things
in you that you can't see in yourself

One day, a young man asked me to think about starting a business partnership with him. He was a former class-mate who graduated before I did. We had several classes together. My first thought was a resounding no. I was afraid. I wasn't as good as he was. We had different mind-sets. He was in his early 20s, without any business expe-rience but talented. I was almost 50, had a small amount of business experience, and was insecure in my abilities. We had a meeting. He said he could see me talking to people, getting clients as well as working on the graphics and websites. He definitely saw more in me than I saw in myself. So we started Level Up Web Designs. I surprised myself. Although I was still in school, we did really well. Unfortunately, the business partnership ended. I took more classes to strengthen me where I was weak and now I'm more confident in running a business for myself.

That wasn't the only business. After my third graduation in 2018, I became a Certified Professional Life Coach. While I was at the school, I was allowed to be an unofficial student coach. I would meet with students to talk about classes, career choices, resumes, and interviewing techniques. They knew that I cared about them and wanted the best for them.

After graduating with my degree in 2020, the school's president offered me a position as the Student Success Coach. He saw something in me that I didn't see myself. He saw how much I cared. The student assigned to me were considered "high-risk." They were having a difficult time with online classes and the pandemic. I was helping them turn their grades from Ds and Fs to As and Bs. I was excited to get paid to do what I came to love. Once I left the school, I began a new coaching business where I work with young adults and with women trying to get their lives back after a traumatic experience. Moving Forward with Nellie Life & Career Coaching was born.

Lesson:

GOD has never given up on you

In February 2002, I was called to the ministry, and 'Singled Out by Design Ministries' was born in New York City. After moving to North Carolina, "SEEP, Sisters of Excellence & Extraordinary Power" was born. I worked with some wonderful women to help them grow spiritually and know GOD. I had monthly meetings, conferences, retreats, and preaching engagements until the stroke. When I couldn't lead as I once had, the ministry dissipated. As I healed, I prayed. That's when GOD opened the door to teach the students at school. When the pandemic happened, Bible study continued online. Once I left the school, I continued teaching young adults from different states via Zoom. Beyond Boundaries, Bible Study was born. Just because I experienced the stroke didn't mean GOD was through with me. I still have the assignment to minister to people. My ministry shifted and I had to shift with it. I was comfortable ministering to the women but now ministering to young adults is totally different. My perspective on preaching was different. My perspective on teaching was different. My perspective on relating to them changed. My perspective on GOD was different, broader, wider, and deeper. Girl, Get Your Life Back is a product of how GOD matured me in this season of my life. Know that GOD can use you in whatever state you are in.

Girl, Get Your
Life Back!

Stroke. No two are the same. No recoveries are the same. No results are the same. Getting your life back is going to look different from woman to woman. It was then I knew I couldn't keep this to myself. I wanted to open it up for other women to tell of their journey. We want to encourage women, men, families, and caregivers that there is life after a stroke. It will take time. It will take effort. It will take determination. It will take strength. It will take introspection. It will take courage. It will also take a lot of tears. You will struggle. You will want to give up. You will yell, holler, and scream. I'm here to tell you it will all be worth it.

Hi, my name is Nellie and I'm an ordained minister, college graduate, Bible study teacher, preacher, workshop facilitator, life coach, career coach, graphic/web designer, entrepreneur, Big Nellie's granddaughter, and Stroke Survivor!

What's next for me?

"No eye has seen,
no ear has heard,
and no mind has imagined
the things that God has prepared
for those who love him." – 1 Cor. 2:9

Cynthia Young

A Boston native, living near Phoenix, Arizona,
a wife, and Stroke Survivor

Cynthia is a Feng Shui practitioner and Trauma Support specialist. She lives a life philosophy based on balanced wellness. Cynthia's history as a Pediatric Stroke Survivor allows her to help others create a regulated and safe environment and celebrate self-compassion as healing.

The past traumas that we continue to experience show up in our living spaces as familiar vehicles of comfort. Together we work to create space for our past fears and shadow to be seen. When Cynthia is not working, she can be found enjoying the splendor of the Southwest desert with her husband and creating crystal grids for healing.

Links to Cynthia's Work and Contact Info:

https://asteyastudios.com/

https://www.instagram.com/asteyastudios_feng_shui/

cynthiayoung.az@gmail.com

(978) 771-1002

A Burning Blessing:

Staying in the Fire with the Mind-Body Connection

Cynthia Young

There is a cool metal feel to the steel of the swing set as I make my way, hand-over-hand across the bars. The brown leaves on the ground crunch as I let go and land. It is a typical New England Fall day with blue sky and leafy trees and I stop to tie my sneaker. There is a whir of energy knowing that the first day of first grade is only one sleep away. That memory is one of many that I have growing up before the age of six. Unknowingly, I was on the threshold of a life that would lead me on a journey of learning to overcome, heal, and find compassion for myself and ultimately for others.

The night before the first day of first grade my mother put me to bed just like any other night. The only remarkable thing I remember, other than the fabric headboard of my bed, which I had scribbled on with a marker, was that I had a headache upon going to sleep. Somewhere in the late hours of that evening, I woke up feeling strange and wet from having lost control of my body functions. Calling for my mom, she stood me up and began attending to the bed. I slumped against my bookcase. Upon seeing my left side go limp and not being able to stand, my mom immediately called the only doctor in the small town of 1,200 people. I will never forget my pediatrician, Dr. Norman Gaudrault, driving to our home and escorting us to a Boston hospital. I recall the dark night sky as we approached the Tobin Bridge in Boston. I was struggling to stay upright and wrapped in a brown Granny-square afghan continually vomiting in the front seat. I recall, without too much detail, my father paying the toll for my doctor, as the Doctor had no wallet; he had driven to our home in his pajamas, not wanting to waste a moment changing clothes. My memory after that is fragmented. I know now that trauma sometimes leaves us with no memories, to help us survive. As our body fights to survive it shuts down the executive function of our brains. What I do remember is the cold feeling of an emergency room with blue masks looking down at me under bright lights.

There was a cascading, filtered light that flowed through the hospital room window. It must have been hours after I was admitted to Boston Children's Floating Hospital. I remember hearing my father's voice and then seeing him collapse in the corner of my room. Nurses attended to him—he had passed out from seeing my small body hooked to monitors and other machines unable to move my left side. On my 20th day in the hospital, I felt a flinch in my left leg. Within a few minutes, I was able to move my left leg off the bed slightly. I called for a nurse who called my mom. This was a big step forward in my recovery and my left arm soon followed in slight movement a few days later. This led to years of physical and occupational therapy.

This was a long way from the original prognosis which suggested to my mother that she should move me to an institution for disabled children because I'd never thrive or walk. This was also the start of a polarized relationship with Western medical providers in general because of the misunderstanding of my body and what it needed. I was released from Boston Floating Hospital after several weeks. I remember arriving home to a cake and blonde brownies made by my aunt Jo. I've never had a blonde brownie that tasted as good as those did.

After many months, the return to the Massachusetts educational system proved challenging. At that time, before consistent support for special needs students, the system was unsure of what to do with a physically disabled child who didn't have a collapse of intellectual skills. I returned to the halls of my elementary school first-grade classroom in a wheelchair. My environmental surroundings from that moment on became about safety. I recognize now, as a trauma support specialist, that my nervous system is always going to scan for threats and mobilize based on all these past experiences. I was tutored for months to make up for the time that I missed and was able to move forward with my class.

At a certain point, my wheelchair became unnecessary. I had learned to walk again with intermittent crutch use and surpassed the expectations of my therapy require-ments. This meant I could be mobile with the aid of a leg brace. You would think the story ends here with me advancing to second grade as a walking, talking seven-year-old. Alas, the story of that life was just beginning.

Without a wheelchair and now walking with a limp, my physical disability can be hard to see. The eventual diagnosis was a left-side ischemic stroke that caused childhood cerebral palsy and left-side hemiplegia. The paralysis is severe on my left side, despite having gained back perhaps 65% of mobility. As someone who spent so much time growing up in recovery and an intense focus on "overcoming" philosophy, I became hyper-vigi-lant and intensely independent. This is a response to my trauma caused by feeling a lack of safety. It was difficult to ask for help. Asking for help was often met with "You can do anything if you try, just like normal kids." This led to feelings of shame. If I needed help, then I must not be trying hard enough. "Shame on me." I remember having a substitute teacher who was unaware of my disability. She mentioned during class that it was almost time for recess. Knowing I could not put on my jacket alone, I raised my hand and begged for her to call on me. I knew I needed extra time and help to get my jacket. Instead of investigating the cause of my urgency, she shunned and shamed me. She told me that I was being disruptive. What I needed were help and extra time. My body was then sent into urgency by the fear of being left behind and unsafe. I was left feeling invalidated and sad. Having a disability that others don't understand is a double-edged sword. Stroke is viewed as an elderly person's disease.

I became a star for learning to walk again, but it made me fiercely independent, which often left me fatigued and unsure of how to make a mistake or ask for help. Once you've done something miraculous like walk, when they told you that you couldn't, you expect that from yourself all the time. I turned into the child that was always the center of attention, quick-witted and agreeable. It was my nervous system trying to control any threat or conflict that felt unsafe. This was the Burning Blessing of my stroke.

The elementary school system was not equipped to deal with bullying in 1975. The awkwardness of wearing a gray AFO brace on my left leg was the inspiration for taunts, name-calling, and physical attacks. I wish, at that time, that someone had taught me how to state my needs and state clearly that I wouldn't accept abusive behavior. My defense against bullies was to laugh it off or engage in "if you can't beat 'em join 'em" behavior and use violent language against me. I think this likely resulted in injury to my self-esteem. One of the phrases I was taught to say was, "Take a picture it will last longer," in response to uncomfortable staring.

Saying this, again and again, was a deflection for stating exactly what my need was—I needed to say, "Your staring makes me feel shunned, please ask a question if you have one." Surviving a traumatic, life-threatening experience is a victory, but the fierce vigilance and isolation it creates are intolerable: it's the Burning Blessing. This behavior didn't change much throughout the rest of my public education experience. I had become an "attractive, nice, quiet girl" which led to my becoming a people pleaser and conflict avoider. At the center of the "pleasant girl" was a wounded heart and a completely unsure and emotionally unsupported child. My childhood was about recovery and pushing forward. What was missing was consolation, compassion, and reassurance/regulation. This caused me to disconnect from my body for many years. Because of the disconnection, I was left with minimizing thoughts in my head which forced me to play small for much of my life.

I was able to identify my own triggers early in my college years. I began to realize that loud sounds, strong smells and shouting would trigger anxiety and if bad enough would trigger a collapse of my emotions. I now know the experience is called Misophonia. Meltdowns and emotional dysregulation were common for me at that time. Despite this, college was a place where I bloomed. Attending a small, private New England College led me to find writing and creative process as a refuge. Using electronics to create, (computers were just coming onto the scene in the late 80s), I found great introspection in writing. I was acknowledged as a writer and was able to create a great circle of peers. This experience went a long way toward strengthening my self-esteem. However, the trauma still present in my body followed me into adulthood consistently. Although I was learning about healing my trauma from childhood, I still didn't understand it fully and my trauma was still in the driver's seat.

Anxiety in my early 20s was at times crushing and led to a slew of toxic employment situations and partnerships. Without healthy self-esteem, we attract people who will gladly take advantage of us. These people mistakenly confirm to us that we deserve less because we are convinced that we are not good enough. Trying to find my voice and who I really was came at a price and I was still treating myself in the most ungrateful and non-gentle behaviors. Trauma can sometimes look like an agreeable, people-pleasing, self-shaming portrait. Couple that with intermittent health issues and the result is a poor support system and crumbling marital dynamic. This is what survival mode looks like. Nourishing yourself with crumbs because it looks resilient, but consistently depleting yourself for the sake of appearing "normal."

My inability to understand and regulate my nervous system led to hyper-vigilant behavior and to my taking on way too many tasks, projects, or work. In my dysregulated body, I was trying to prove that I could keep up with all the "normal people" and that I could do it better than everyone expected. Behavior like this, which was a direct result of my body being in fight or flight, caused extreme fatigue, severe emotional waves, and constant illness. For a medical trauma survivor, the philosophy is, "if I'm not first, I'm last". There is the fear of being left behind and abandoned.

I'm reminded of a quote that I read much later in my life by the author and psychologist, Dr. Bessel Van Der Kolk: "The human brain is a social organ that is shaped by experience, and that is shaped in order to respond to the experience that you're having. So particularly earlier in life, if you're in a constant state of terror; your brain is shaped to be on alert for danger, and to try to make those terrible feelings go away." (Childhood Trauma Leads to Brains Wired for Fear)

Much of what I write in this chapter from here on will be about discovering my trauma response patterns and triggers and how I rebuilt my personal relationships and my self-worth. Please stay along with me: It took the instructor probably three years to get me into the small studio, maybe longer. Finally, with a bit of sharp wit and a keenly caring heart, the owner of the small yoga studio convinced me that yoga and meditation would help me heal and learn to love myself. As I became aregular attendee, he became a treasured mentor. In my early 30's, I had been living a life of self-attack, poor self-worth, and compulsive behaviors. All of this was to fill the space that my dysregulated nervous system was creating. The trauma of my stroke caused an inability to regulate my emotions and I often wavered between high highs and very low lows. To fill the space of unhappiness and low self-worth I behaved in ways that would get my attention regardless of the consequences. I felt invisible because of my disability and loudly announced any success so that I could get attention, and someone would say, "Good job." If only someone would have said, "I see you, you're working hard," but that support system didn't exist at that moment. Once I began teaching meditation at the studio, I learned breathing techniques that allowed me to sink with kindness into my body. I learned to befriend my body and the emotions that were the result of my fight-or-flight survival mode. The "good job" I so desperately craved soon came from inside me. My meditation practice became a nightly ritual. This proved to be the foundation I need for healing.

I want to stop right here and say that now as a trauma support professional, I only recommend breathing techniques that are appropriate for each unique individual. Measured breathing and mindfulness can be triggering to some clients with trauma. In my case, it was highly effective. I sat against the wall of my bedroom and set a timer for 15 minutes. Next to me, I adorned a small altar with items that I loved. I sat in silence with no goal. I just sat, eyes closed, breathing. After several weeks I noticed that my surroundings started to get "cleaned up." The small apartment where I was now living alone became more organized and I was attending to things like laundry, closets, and kitchen storage. The more I sat in meditation, the less sporadic I was. I became more attuned to my body and my present-day life. The big realization here is that trauma keeps us frozen in the past. A mindful practice like meditation allowed me to focus on the present moment. I will again stress that breathing techniques have to be personalized so as not to retraumatize a survivor.

Another practice that I began at this time was gratitude writing. I would sit every morning with a pen, paper, and a basket. I would write whatever I was grateful for that day. Soon, I had an overflowing basket. When you are living alone after the divorce and trying to make part-time money stretch, sometimes gratitude is: "I'm grateful for gas money," "I'm grateful for food shopping," and "I'm grateful for the ease of breath today." Practicing true gratitude kept unhealthy thoughts from being prominent. Again, I must pause and say that Western culture has misappropriated the concept of gratitude. It is sometimes used as a shaming mechanism; "You should be grateful nothing worse happened," or "Be grateful because other people have it worse." It doesn't work as the self-help teachers tell you and it is invalidating and bypassing.

Gratitude means you stand in front of the mirror and find self-love regardless of flaws or process. Gratitude is affirmative prayer where you don't strive to change or be "better", you just step into the fullness of who you are. You always have an opportunity to show up as however you are in the moment. Every moment is an opportunity to show yourself compassion. Negative thoughts, struggling, and financial concern, are not failures; they are an opportunity to learn and hold yourself gently in process. The truth is being disabled is very painful and filled with fatigue and dysregulation. But I step into the world in that fullness of being tired, hurt and willing to love myself even if I'm in pain. The idea of recovery and resiliency isn't to eradicate pain and deny disability, it is to touch it tenderly again and again to become familiar with it. We're not attempting to integrate pain, but to acknowledge it and its need for self-compassion.

The best thing I did during my years alone was to get friendly with money. For many trauma survivors, including stroke, the process of managing finances can be overwhelming. It is difficult enough to manage your already dysregulated nervous system; money management after a stroke is daunting. I think the difficulty lies in learning to see your finances as a whole—to view each financial transaction and bill paying without fear. I worked part-time after my divorce in 2013 and learned to make my money work: in addition to my gratitude work, I learned to understand that finances are cyclical-that when there is an ebb, there is an eventual flow. I had to remember that every time I paid a bill, wrote a check, or got gas. My money balance would get low, but through my intention and action, the balance would go up again. Finances are connected to our immediate energy. If we are living in gratitude and living in the present, finances can be managed. The Universe always shows up with money if you ask for it in a mindful way.

I met my current husband in 2015 and after a brief time together we made the move cross country to the southwest. Life became abundant here and many of the intentions I set during my gratitude work manifested. It was here that I became a Feng Shui consultant. All my study of meditation and doing the work to survive a life transition began to flow. It was in moving to Arizona that I realized I had previously been adjusting my behavior to suit other people's needs. I had still been living as that "pleasant, agreeable six-year-old girl" and I was not making my needs known. Setting up our new home and putting in place healthy boundaries for each other and the people closest to us allow us to live in a harmonized environment. After trauma, the nervous system will try to keep you in a marathon of dysregulated behavior to keep you safe; resting or change in behaviors often feel risky and unsafe as we learn to regulate. The pace in the southwest is much slower and there is an opportunity to get present in the now of life. I am far better at using my toolbox to help regulate my nervous system. I still feel trauma responses daily and my body wants to remind me that as a small girl, I almost died. That will never change, but the pause between trigger and response gets wider.

To begin to live a thriving life not locked into my stroke history took a lot of hard work. It required understanding that because I almost died, my body is always going to attempt to keep me safe. And when my body senses something unsafe, it's going to react. It's going to want to flee, fight or freeze. Learning to pause before reacting and getting present with what I'm feeling is the key. Now in each situation, I can say, "My body is reacting because I don't feel safe and that is bringing big intense emotion."

It helps that I have a partner who also understands my

body's natural retreat from danger. He acts as a co-regulator for me. There are times when I have to leave the grocery store and sit in the car because it's crowded or I see people in my peripheral (the body only needs to sense a threat for it to mobilize, there doesn't have to be a real threat) or the music may be too loud and overwhelming. I am now very good at stating my needs: we become low in self-worth and exhausted when we don't say exactly what we need. People in our lives are not mind readers and most times are not going to "figure out" what we need. Stating a need might be something like, "It's very loud in here and I feel my body reacting. I'm going to sit in the car while you finish shopping," or "I'm feeling depleted today, so if we could have this conversation a bit later, I'll be better able to participate," or "I am really anxious that we are running late, it feels unsafe when we have to rush" or simply "I really enjoy the time with you when I have your full attention. I feel seen."

For my nervous system to be regulated and not deplete me, I need transition time between moments in my day. I build in slow, mindful moments to process a phone call, appointment, or task. Because my nervous system will always feel like fleeing, it will try to rush me through my day. It will try to quickly move me from task to task in an attempt to reduce the threat. To redirect this mobilization, I use the breathing techniques I've taught over the years for myself and have also learned techniques like tapping, EMDR, swaddling, and other somatic exercises. I also still work my gratitude practice, although in a bit of a different way. Most of all, I accept the support and love that is given to me because I feel worthy and because I don't tolerate anything less than that feeling for myself now.

Consider for a moment what I've said about stroke being a burning blessing. It's our job as stroke survivors to slow down and be present with our bodies. It is our job to recognize our body's mobilization for survival. Healing isn't necessarily a big emotional process; it is a consistent movement toward understanding what our capacity is and where our resiliency is born. Resiliency is born from the times we slip back into dysregulation and then know how to become regulated again and again and again. We practice with our bodies every day so that when a bad day arrives, we are ready to cope, use our tools and remember our worthiness. I recently learned to invite that six-year-old girl into a thriving life. She deserves to be acknowledged, seen, and cared for. Together, we are warmed by the burning blessing.

Angela Papoutsakis

Colombian, resident of New Jersey.
Wife of George Papoutsakis and mother of
Aristides, Sofia and Michelle.

Angela is a bestselling Author, Speaker, Lecturer, International Chaplain, Human Rights Consultant, Certified in Emotional Intelligence, The Art of Public Speaking, Volunteer, and she's a Leader in Diverse, Press, and Radio Correspondent for Exploit Miami, and a Stroke Survivor.

Her bestselling book: Love, the Medicine for Disease, was nominated for the Latino Diamonds Awards.

Co-author of three books, and two are in Spanish, one book of poetry and one devotional book. Soon her book, Love, Medicine for Illness, will be in English.

Life before
the Stroke

My name is Angela, I was born in Colombia, and I currently live in the State of New Jersey for almost 30 extraordinary years; my parents are Hernando and Ligia and I'm the fifth of seven sisters. My childhood was delightful between the two cities of Cali and Bogota, Colombia. I was surrounded by my grandparents, parents, sisters, aunts, uncles, cousins, as well as my many friends, and teachers; there were ups and downs, but I had incredible memories that I will carry in my heart forever.

When I was eight years old, I attended a ballet school where my sister, Alicia, and I studied. As I passed all my exams, that allowed me to have the opportunity to study at a unique ballet school, Incolballet. During the mornings I would attend artistic subjects such as ballet, piano, voice choir, music, theater, corporal expression, art history, folklore and contemporary dance; and in the afternoons I would study the academic parts: mathematics, Spanish, French and science. There I obtained the degree of *Bachelor of Artistic Ballet.*

I graduated in the summer of 1988, with my last performance being the Nutcracker. I was the leading dancer. It took plenty of hardworking hours of rehearsing, but in the end it was all worth it. While getting ready to perform for the gala, my choreographer Clara Carranco, who was in charge of preparing Álvaro and I, my partner in duet or in French, "pas de deux", who is now the director of ballet in Washington DC. Carranco was a professor at the school and company of National Ballet in Cuba. She was strict, demanding a lot from us because she saw the potential in each and every one of us; always wanting us to be excellent in the classical technique she taught us, she constantly pushed me to do the best I could, motivating me to keep going. What beautiful memories, and tears!

I would absolutely love to be able to embrace the eight classmates during graduation again, for so many great moments experienced, and memories of us fooling around. One memory was when one of my classmates, Maria, who illegally drove a bus with students inside of it for fun, me being one of them. The vice principal chased after all of us on a motorcycle with the security in our school attempting to stop Maria. Another silly moment I think back to was when we would hide in the bathrooms and arrive with candy under our leotards. We would do this in the class with one of the best masters, Zaraspe, who came all the way from the Juilliard School in New York to teach us his magnificent work and skills.

He passed away recently, and I cannot thank him enough for everything he did for us. Zaraspe, I will continuously carry you within my heart. I learned so much about the discipline of ballet from you that I will treasure for the rest of my life.

Another person I would like to acknowledge and thank is teacher Amparo, she taught us Spanish, I remember her always encouraging us to read and write. Every time I sit down and write, she is someone I look back on.

These were years full of learning, traveling, having great teachers, and great friends who have a very important place in my heart.

After graduating from high school, I was able to take big trips that marked my life with the ballet company. I like to describe these trips with a lot of modesty, being humble about all my experiences. Flying to Paris was a dream come true, where we danced at UNESCO, (The United Nations Educational, Scientific, and Cultural Organization). There were countless of other journeys too, likewise, participating in the International Ballet Festival in La Habana, Cuba, Aruba, Puerto Rico, and other locations. It was a privilege to meet one of the best dancers in the world, Alicia Alonso, as well as great teachers, and choreographers around the world.

I joined the Ballet Company, and I took classes in Pedagogy for teaching ballet for the first and second year. I was a ballet instructor at the school where I graduated. I also studied English at Icesi, which is a university in Colombia. I worked in other companies and also taught ballet and dance at the Anna Pávlova Ballet School and the German School in Cali, Colombia.

The discipline of ballet and all my artistic and academic training had given me a great basis for what I am now; the arduous rehearsals, the trips, and having to comply with the academic parts. Doing homework was a daily routine,while on Saturdays and Sundays were rehearsals. Trips would be for long periods of time within the span of a month or two. Great memories and lessons that I will never forget.

I decided to come to the United States to continue with my studies. I took classes in ballet companies and schools in New York. I had many jobs to pay for all the expenses. One of them being with an airline where I was sent to Houston, Texas (when the airline tickets were hand-made); I also worked in clothing stores, I sold makeup, and also worked in a supermarket. I did everything to pay for my ballet classes.There were good moments and others not so good, but all of them were great experiences that have brought me where I am today.

I found myself in another culture, even though I had already come to the United States several times thanks to the Ballet, it was not the same to come for longer than I usually would, settling down permanently to start a new life, as you must learn so much being an Immigrant.

Leaving your country is not easy, but I bless this Nation for all that it has given me. Today I am a proud American citizen and have lived more than half of my life in this great country. Here I met George, my now husband who is a Greek man who is insanely hardworking, and a wonderful father to my three children: Aristides, Sofia, and Michelle. We moved to live near the sea because of my husband's business, which was a fast-food restaurant, which sold Greek food and had an ice cream parlor.

Little by little we were raising the business and it was growing, lots of years of hard work, where we could share with great human beings. During the winter we were able travel when the kids were young, going to Greece, Colombia, and Canada, visiting both me and my husband's families.

George fell in love with Colombia because of its mountains, and its two oceans: the Atlantic and the Pacific; the food and the people. At the same time, I fell in love with Greece, the island of Karpathos where my husband was born. Honestly, I had never seen landscapes like those of Amoopi, a landmark where his sister has a restaurant. From his apartment I could see the whole Mediterranean Sea so close from the windows. The water had beautiful colors that looked like a big pool without waves, seriously, if one day you could travel to Greece, you need to visit Karpathos Island. It has great beaches, you can enjoy

Mediterranean food that is spectacular, and understand their culture. You can also have the opportunity to visit the Parthenon, and its museums. What beautiful memories with Aristo and Sofia, who are my husband's parents and all of his other family. It is difficult to describe in words, but how gorgeous are all the wonderful creations of God?

Karpathos is the second largest island of the Dode Canese, (twelve islands) and is located between Rhodes and Crete. It was recently named one of the twelve most beautiful islands in the whole world to visit.

My husband, children and I long so much to go back, but due to my husband's health issues and life circumstances, him battling cancer has made it a struggle to go back, but we know that God has the perfect timing ready for us to go again, so my husband can see his mother and his whole family.

The Stroke

Two tragic events occurred that marked a before and an after in our lives in 2012, which was one of the most heartbreaking years for me and my family.

Everything seemed to be going very well; we expanded the business by putting up an arcade which held video games for the children, and a clothing and beach store right next door to the restaurant.

I remember that day vividly, July 18, 2012, as if it was yesterday. I worked all day helping my husband, there were a lot of people on the beach and in the store, the weather was around 100 degrees, and I went to rest for a little while to take a break and see my children. I remember I was feeling very tired and my head was hurting a little.My niece came to visit us and told me that we should take the children for a walk on Boardwalk in Seaside to enjoy sightseeing and games, but I asked her to take them because I was feeling exhausted and wanted to sleep, and my eyes were slowly closing. She told me not to worry that she would take them, so they left and I stayed back.

The hours passed, and I only heard when they came back, but I continued sleeping. And everything started before 12:00 A.M. I heard my son trying to tell me that he was hungry, which was rare at that time, because he used to open the fridge or ask for food upstairs, where my husband was. When I heard my son tell me, "Mommy I'm hungry", I wanted to turn around, but I couldn't, I wanted to talk, but I couldn't, I wanted to think, but it felt like an atomic bomb was in my brain.

I invite you to close your eyes, to not breathe for some minutes. It is something horrible, oxygen doesn't reach your brain, you want to run away, scream, and you can't; there are involuntary movements that you have no control over.

A Stroke is very traumatic, and I still remember it and I can't stop crying as I write these lines, because it is something beyond description. It is a feeling of helplessness that sweeps over you, and you don't know what is happening to your body. I remember that I was sweating as if I had taken a bath. Every second that passes is crucial, you are between life and death, and if you do not act in time, you can die or else your incapacities can be worse. Seeing my son's face of terror, feeling the tears running down my face and me still unable to speak, I only heard him shouting and questioning "Mom! Mom! Are you okay?"

My son ran to be the first to call 911. The police and para-medics arrived, and at that moment they gave me injections in my stomach, and some things on my chest that I couldn't identify, I was put on a stretcher and taken away to the hospital. By that time, my husband and the rest of my family had already come down, I only remember the image of their faces full of sadness and concern as they did not understand what was happening to me.

It was so terrible as if one part of my body was leaving and the other was fighting to stay. How much pain in my mind to see my husband and my three children like that - it all happened so fast, and my son was like an angel, because the doctor told me that if my son had not come to wake me, I would have died. The doctor explained that when he woke me up, I was having a stroke in my sleep, the clot burst between my neck and my brain and at that specific moment, if my son hadn't come to wake me, I would be dead. He said that it was almost as if something told him to wake me up, like a sign from God. After hearing all of this, I hysterically cried, not understanding why I had to go through that, but thanking the Lord that I was still alive.

Thank God for this new opportunity of life, there is a before and an after, because my heart suffered. The doctors had to put a special device in my heart. You get very weak as if a hurricane and an atomic bomb had exploded in your brain. I wanted to stand up and I fell, I had no strength, my balance was compromised, and there were very difficult days of great pain and agony. I had not managed to recover when on October 28, 2012, Sandy, the super hurricane came and we lost everything we had -absolutely, everything.

Recovering From My Stroke

It was a double blow for me, because on one hand I was battling for my health, and on the other hand I was dealing with losing everything, from our home, to our business. Going through these difficult moments, I went to my knees, and with tears I asked God to help me begging to give me courage, that he would give me the strength to stand up, because it was no longer with my strength that I would do it, but with His. My husband was depressed, and my children were suffering. Intertwining our hands, and as a family we began to walk together, and in resilience to rise from all that had been going on; from the human to the supernatural, we walk by faith, because today we rise stronger than ever, and we know that life can put you the hardest and most difficult tests. I assure you that you can get up, and that after the rain it always leads to sunshine; and if it is not your day or your hour, your purpose is fulfilled and they are no longer my plans, they are God's plans for my life. I had to tell my brain many times that I would be fine, the "no's" would become "yes's" and tell my mind and heart, "Yes, you can do it, Angela! Disabilities are in your mind, with God everything is possible, you are a miracle and if you stayed alive it was to have a different life with dreams and goals with a purpose."

Besides God, there were two very important people to whom I will be eternally grateful, the neurologist, Dr. Sarris, and the cardiologist, Dr. Moussa. The two of them together, along with God, never let go of my hand. They gave me confidence and strength for my recovery, and they promised that they would always be alongside me, and they were.

When I was able to start moving, my life took a turn. I started attending emotional healing meetings and courses, as well as public speaking courses. I needed to get acquainted with the new me, the person who was a stroke survivor, the person who suddenly had to look at the world with different eyes. With the eyes of someone who was about to lose everything, but recovered it, with patience, with love from my loved ones; nourishing myself all the time to start over. Thanks to all that, I can tell my story.

After my recovery, I began to dedicate my life to helping others, to have empathy for those who suffer, for those who lose, because let me tell you that, yes, there are material things, but what matters is your life and how you spend your days. One cannot ask themself, "Why is this happening to me?" However, we are to say, "Everything happens for a reason." I never thought this would happen to me. l would like to tell you anything is possible, and you never know what day will be your last, and the next could be you.

Every second and every day is a blessing, that in the ordinary, in the simple, with little or with a lot you can achieve many things. I never imagined that I would write a book and that it would become a best seller. The story of my life, "El Amor: La Medicina Para la Enfermedad" which translates to "Love: The Medicine for Illness". God planted it in my heart so that someone will rise like me. Our dreams are not extinguished by what has happened to us, by what we were, what was done to us or what happened.Neither traumas nor illnesses define us.

This is my third book collaboration, but one of the most important with resilient women who have suffered and are survivors of a Stroke. What a beautiful gift of life! I could not be more grateful and blessed. The best is yet to come, just like me, you can be lifted too by celebrating every little step of the way, you can do this all at your own pace and in your own time. It is okay to cry, but don't be discouraged and instead be encouraged to tell your story and live a legacy in this world of love, if I could, you can too, and the sky is the limit.

Either you sit down to cry and be depressed, or you rise - this is your season to shine, to conquer. Girl, get your life back.

Shawnnett Gaines

A native of the Bronx, New York. She is a three-time stroke survivor. She is a mother of two young men, Jacob and Jarius, and the grandmother of a grandson and granddaughter. Previously, she was a substance abuse counselor and is an ordained minister who truly loves God. She found out her body was under attack and she has protein S deficiency; clotting of the blood. She could no longer eat iron-enriched foods but maybe once or twice a year. After the strokes, she now understands that she is responsible for the gift of life that God has given to her. He gives us knowledge, wisdom, and understanding, and it's up to us if we take heed for our body's sake; eating healthy and exercising consistently are on her list. Her faith rises over every obstacle she faces.

Shawnnett Gaines

Romans 5:1-5

"1. Therefore, being justified by faith, we have peace with God through our Lord Jesus Christ: 2. By whom also we have access by faith into this grace wherein we stand and rejoice in hope of the glory of God. 3. And not only so, but we glory in tribulations also: knowing that tribulation worketh patience; 4. And patience, experience, and experience, hope: 5. And hope makes not ashamed; because the love of God is shed abroad in our hearts by the Holy Ghost which is given unto us."

I am responsible with this gift of life that God has given to me, I understand this now. Life is not to be taken for granted. You did not give it, nor do you have the authority to take it away. Even we as parents must be careful about the life of a child because we may have committed the act which causes a child to be born, we still don't have the power to give life or take it away. Unfortunately, I truly did not know what that meant when I was younger. God was watching out over my life long before I knew I needed Him. My parents (father mother) were reckless and irresponsible, yet I never blamed them for the life that was given to me. God placed me in the care of my loving grandparents and that is where I received the nurturing I needed. That didn't mean that life didn't come with problems, it did, but I was able to overcome them. I overcame the obvious things, but I still took things for granted. Warning sign after warning sign to change my behavior and my eating habits came to me over the years, but I didn't care because being a big girl didn't matter, why, because my grandmother (father's mother) made being a big girl; look so fabulous. She brought nice clothes, she had a man, she had a house, and a good job. It all looked wonderful. The devil had a trap set for me, so he thought. But the grace of God rescued me from my self- indulgent behavior.

Size didn't matter to me, what or how I ate didn't matter to me, what I liked, was what I liked, and I refused to change, that was the stubborn side of me. I didn't realize the Lord was letting me see the negative side as well as the positive side of things. I saw life as a puzzle, and we were getting by, by our wits, thank God for intellect. Well, I took life and my health for granted up until the age of 45 and at 45 it changed me changed for me, and the opportunity to change on my own strength was taken away. It was when I had my first stroke, one of three, came over me. Yes, I'm a three-time stroke survivor. I had work to do, and it has taken the mercy of God to show me I can't do this work on my own. Strong, independent, no-nonsense women surrounded me all my life. They had their flaws, but it didn't detour the love they had instilled in me. Let us remember no one is perfect but Jesus Christ, the rest of us take one day at a time, and one moment at a time and one issue at a time. These strong women showed and showered me with love, but their flaws overshadowed the love they gave to me. The flaws they possessed were their own personal shortcomings and their shortcomings were little roadblocks for me.

I realized that this life that God gave me is not really my own. Meaning it is not mine to abuse, use or do with what I want. My life is to bring glory to God.

2 Timothy 3:16-17

"All scripture is breathed out by God and profitable for teaching, for reproof, for correction, and for training in righteousness, that the man of God may be competent, equipped for every good work."

What I say, what I do, even how I feel is essential to the testimony of what God has done in my life. Does that mean that I have no say in what I do, of course not, what that means is I should seek the wisdom of God on each direction I should go on? God gives us independence, yes, but what do we do with it, and what we want personally, for ourselves, are different things. Our wants can cloud our vision, and it can cloud our mind on what is more important, and that is to glorify God. All that being stated I must say all the regrets I have, is not failing, we will all fail at something, even worse we fail at the same thing more than once. What is worse than failing, it's not trying. You'll never know if you can or cannot do something if you don't try. Fail or succeed is only the outcome when you try to meet the challenge. I believe that each stroke that I had was a warning sign given to me that, I was supposed to live. Despite whatever happened, I lived – Hallelujah! Like Bro. Job, he was tested and not killed. He was left here to declare the glory of God despite terrible misfortunate happenings. There are some things that I do want to do or want to have, but they are purely selfish reasons? The hardest realities I have had to face are, or my motives pure and in the end will God get the glory, or will I?

During this time of healing God has given me time to reflect on the lives I've touched, the people I've met, and the experiences I've had made. I'm truly grateful for all I've done up until this moment. Each stroke has slowed me down, it has given me time to reflect and to record all that God has taken me through. I have had to learn things all over again, from eating - what an experience, dressing, walking, and even thinking. It has been a struggle, some things came easy, some things I still struggle with only because I know what I was once able to do with ease, and now I'm not. My hindrances are where my struggles take root. On one hand, the strokes I had help me receive benefits that pay my expenses with ease, and without this assistance, living in New York would be a struggle. Since my walking has slowed down greatly, I am limited to where I can go and how long it will take me to get there. The 24-hour assistance I receive would go away, if I dare to do something on my own or decide to go away, it would limit the benefits I would receive, so stepping outside of this box of convenience is a blessing and a curse.

In getting my life back to normal, it is to define what normal looks like for me.

1. Does my life line up with the Word of God? Not per say, but figuratively. How does the Word of God sound to me?
2. Does the Word of God sound the same coming from me? Envision and list out my accomplishments, and go in line with the leading of the Holy Ghost.
3. Learn how to interact with others more effectively, and not being afraid to conversate and to pray more.
4. Listening more intensely, and speaking clear and precise. Making prayer a primary focus in my life.
5. Exercise consistently.

You must always remember the devil does not care about your physical limitations, nor does he care about what you do or don't have, the only thing he cares about is your belief system and if you proclaim it as well as live it. Normal looks different to everyone based on what was afforded to them and what they have acquired over time. Everyone has selfish motives, (everyone has needs they want to have met) not everyone acts on their selfish motives though, but they become clear if you or anyone interrupts the goals intended. However, in order to reach my goals, my dreaded nemesis must take place; change. Change has got to take place in my life. I like things to stay simple and the same. I want my family and friends to be happy, and for the situations in my life to work out smoothly, but that isn't always realistic. Why, because life happens, and it is not prescribed by man. God is in control, and I want to follow peace like the scripture declares, but each situation for someone else is different.

Hebrews 12:14

"Follow peace with all men, and holiness, without which no man shall see the Lord."

In the beginning, after my first stroke, did I reflect on why I ended up this way? Now in trying to get my life back I realize that you can't just do what you want and expect everything to go your way. I love to read the Old Testament, for me it is a teaching tool. All throughout the first five books especially as it speaks about what sin could do. I say all this because we as a people need guidance, instructions, and the leading of the Holy Ghost. Our thoughts lead us astray before our actions will. Now the scripture tells us what we should eat and why. It also notes that everything God has made is good, and for ministering purposes we should not be limited.

1 Corinthians 10:25

"Eat whatever is sold in the meat market without raising any question on the ground of conscience"

I thought I could eat whatever I wanted to eat, and nothing would happen to me. How wrong was my thinking? I took this life of mine for granted and ate whatever pleased me, even if I knew it was not good for me. Now because of my reckless self- indulgence I'm forced to be mindful; what I eat, how much of what I eat and what time I eat it. I can't eat everything anymore; everything must be eaten in moderation. Just because it tastes good to me doesn't mean it's good for me to eat it. I now must be mindful of what goes into my body. I do indulge in some of my favorite foods, but I don't eat in excess anymore. For instance, I love rice, any way you can make rice, just put it in a bowl, give me spoon and it's all over. However, rice spikes my sugar rapidly and excessively and since I'm diabetic and sugar is a major factor to my strokes, I can't eat it anymore. Two to three tablespoons tops is all that I can eat now. Most of my favorite foods are starchy and bad for my sugar; now I know what small portions mean and eating in moderation.

I love me, I have always loved me, and I still love me. I have never wanted to hurt or abuse myself; but in getting my life back to some type of normalness I see where food was the way I mistreated myself. Food didn't talk back or argue. Food, good food, did not give me problems. Thus, I made food the way I escaped from anything that was hectic and troublesome. I adore good food, and I love to cook, which is funny because, when I was young and my grandmother was trying to teach me how to cook, I got dangerously burned; thus, I didn't go back into the kitchen to cook again until I was thirteen years of age. I'd wash dishes, mop the floor, put the groceries away, but I would not cook. I grew into an excellent cook when I went to live with my mother. Once I learned that, more than I was eating the food, and everybody had different tastes, and I was made to cook for the household, cooking became an enjoyment, a tool in a strong sense. Today, I'll watch you cook, but I don't cook like I use to because I'm learning to control what I indulge in, but I don't like everybody's cooking. Now before I had my strokes, I was active and involved in many projects, but it didn't stop the way I ate, which was my downfall.

I have encountered many people, saved as well as unsaved, those that go to church as well as the non-church goers, and what I have learned is that people are people no matter where you go, and who you meet. The greatest tool for me in this great army that God has assembled is prayer. Prayer is my greatest weapon, my spiritual bow and arrow, my spear but please tell me why food was always involved in many social activities. Despite all I learned, strokes and all I realized God has been by my side and he has kept me. When I should have; could have; would have been dead, He kept me alive. Prayer is the key and faith has unlocked many sealed doors. In my Christian walk I have found the way I solved problems was to eat. In my young-adult days, people cooked for the masses thus not so much the way they liked it for themselves, but the way they knew others would enjoy it, and it was not bland either. I knew this brother in Christ, we had and still have a wonderful friendship, but I always took pictures for different events in front of a plate of food. When he and others got good photos of me, all you would see was a plate of food. Today I don't eat like I use to, and I don't take photos like I use to.

In getting my life back in order, I've gotten this revelation; God made food for me to live, but He didn't create me to love to eat or to live my life focused on food. Wow, I've heard this many times before, in many different arenas, but never applied it to myself, no matter how big I had become. Why am I talking so much about food? Because I made food my focus, and the better it was, the more I made and ate. I even made food a part of the ministry that I provided for the church and the homeless. Today I no longer see food that way, having the strokes helped move that process right along. I still enjoy good food, but it doesn't hold my attention like it has done in times past. If my love for food wasn't so blatant, I would have taken better care of myself, and I may not have had these strokes. Yes, the strokes have slowed me down greatly, but it has also given me the time to gather my mind and focus. It has given me a whole new host of people to engage with. Before the strokes my focus was things that helped others come into the knowledge of Christ, but now I'm taking a little time for myself to stay alive.

Food is not the primary reason people have strokes; there

can be an array of issues, but that wasn't my experience. Food plays an essential part to my experience with the strokes I had. I am a snacker and not the healthy kind. I ate all kinds of junk food throughout my life. That was my first problem. I ate iron enriched foods which is good if your body could digest it well, and I found I my body couldn't, which caused blood clots in my leg, via stroke. The second stroke told me I was Protein S deficient, which means I am unable to eat iron enriched foods, but I now take iron pills to balance my need for iron intake. I was told I was too heavy and if I lost a sufficient amount of weight, I would be healthier and would probably not have more strokes, so I agreed. It was suggested for me to have Bariatric surgery, the sleeve procedure, where they would remove a portion of my stomach. I had to see a psychologist so I could prove that I was mentally ready for this type of surgical procedure. I was ready, but what I was not ready for was the "You can't(s)" You can't eat starchy foods, but you can eat more iron enriched foods. I couldn't eat iron enriched foods because I'm Protein S deficient and it would cause my blood to clot. Certain other foods I may eat once or twice a year, but it will not be on a regular basis. I even went to various nutrition-ists that suggested different ways for me to eat, but to no avail. When I was a child, I was a picky eater; first, food couldn't touch on the plate, no mixing food, or letting it run into one another. It got so bad that my grandmother invested in those plates that had separate sections so my food wouldn't touch. My grandmother used to say it's going to get mixed together in your belly, so what's the problem? I told her, that's not the problem, it had to get past my tongue first, and it must taste right. I have grown out of that. Secondly, there were certain foods I would not eat no matter what. I thank God for ketchup, mustard, and Tupperware divided plates.

The doctors wanted me to eat like a vegan, and that worked for about a year. I then got mad. Why? Because I still had another stroke. "Why, oh God, why me?" Was the question I asked, not because it couldn't happen to me, but more so "God, I made all these changes and for what?!" I lost about seventy pounds over the past years but gained it all back during the pandemic. Remember, I adored grandma as a big gal, and she made it look fantastic. Too bad I ignored the deadly signs, or was ignorant to the fact that some of her ailments was because of her weight. She thought if you weren't big enough or had more than enough to eat, you were malnourished. She even took me to the doctor because she thought I was too thin. She was a big southern cook who fried almost everything, and we had rice, mash potatoes, macaroni and cheese, stewed corn with fat back, and slab bacon, pies, cakes, and so much more. We ate very well, she was sure of that. I didn't really gain weight until after I had my first son. Now I'm changing the way I eat and how I see food differently. This is not because food is bad, but for me, the love of food is like the love of money. It is the root of all evil. Food was not or is not evil, but how I used food to escape my problems was evil. If you would upset me, I would eat, if you argue with me, I would eat food. If I had a problem, then I would cook, then I would eat. I would even feed you so we could eat together.

1 Timothy 6:10

"For the love of money is the root of all evil: which while some coveted after they have erred from the faith and pierced themselves through with many sorrows."

Now let me repeat this, "I love me, why because I was very loved, undeniably loved, sometimes I felt too loved. I never felt unappreciated, I was never abused, nor did I lack anything. I didn't understand paternal love, until I had my own children and saw what a sacrificial life was all about. I wish children came with an instruction book, but praise the Lord they don't, and no two children are alike. What I thought children should automatically know, because I knew it, was not realistic, and my children let me know that in their own special way. They used to make me shake my head in disbelief. My children knew they were loved; however special attention was what they desired from me. For a while I thought they made deals with the devil himself, just to drive me crazy. On top of that, I lost my job and there was no one to help me with the rent or to pay my bills. When things got bad, I turned to snacks. Snacks tasted good, unhealthy snacks tasted very good, and filled a void they never should have. No one asked me if they could help me, nor did I confess that I was going through my own issues. In this Christian walk I tried to never complain, nor did I explain what was going on with me. I didn't give way to the devil in any place, nor did I ease my stress. What I did was stuff my feelings and problems, and by hiding them or putting them off, I was destroying my body from the inside out. I refused to suffer from an inferiority complex, at any age. If you didn't want to help me through my problems, I would figure it out myself. If you don't like me, well I'll be moving right along. Now that's not to say I didn't want any help, or anyone to be my friend, what person doesn't want that. Realistically I was so aware of this fact I kept my friend list to the bare minimal and realized that people come and go. Food became one of my biggest and best friend. Now in bringing some normalness back to my life it may be long and hard, buy by God's grace I intend to do it. I have no one to blame, no regrets but a lot of self-forgiveness and an open mind needed to mend.

Jeremiah 17:7

"Blessed is the man that trusts in the Lord, and whose hope the Lord is."

In my quest for getting my life back to normal, I must believe past my physical limitations and what my body says it is and isn't possible to do. What I do know, if you don't use it, even when it hurts, you will lose the activity to use it. I learnt that from the first stroke I had, and as my condition worsened by the third stroke, I believed it became obvious. I didn't need to be inspired at first but as time went on, and things became more difficult, inspiration was much needed. My hopes to be healed did not need to be diminished, no matter how numb my limbs had become. From the nursing home to living on my own, you would have thought it would have gotten easier; however, it has become more trying. Through the tests of time, how tempted you can get when things don't go your way, and the strangest things come to pass when you least expect it. God blesses you when you are not looking for that blessing. You can pray for days, weeks, months, years, even decades, but who can know the timing of God. In the book of John, in the New Testament of the bible, **John 9:1-7,** the disciples asked the Lord, "Why was this man born blind?" Jesus answered them "This happened so the power of God could be seen." The man could have been mad that he had to deal with this condition, or he could have played the blame game asking what or who was the reason for this blindness, but that was not described in the scripture. The point is, it was so that God could be glorified at that moment and at that time. Now the man didn't know the blessing was coming the way that it did, and in obedience it manifested, and God was praised. Time didn't matter, fault didn't matter, Jesus needed to get the attention of those around Him and He did it, right on time. God wants to heal you and He wants to manifest His love towards you, but He is not governed by your time.

The love of God is so vast and so complex we can't contain it all in a box for us alone to possess. The love of God must be spread abroad to all we encounter, so that when you don't expect it, it comes back to you.

1 John 4:17-19 NKJV

"Love has been perfected among us in this: that we may have boldness in the Day of Judgment; because as He

is, so are we in this world. There is no fear in love; but perfect love casts out fear because fear involves torment. But he who fears has not been made perfect in love. We love Him because He first loved us."

God loves you, He has put that love inside of you, for you to spread to those who need to feel real love. The miracle is when you experience the love that He gives back to you, just because you loved Him and want others to know Him like you knew Him. In getting my life back in order, I've forgotten love was a key instrument to my faith. I'm justified for no other reason than that because I believe. The just shall live by faith, and we ought not to waver in the promises of God with or human disbeliefs but be strengthened in faith by giving glory to God and being fully convinced that what God has promised He will also perform it. In this life or the next (eternal). We need to show one another how to love. God "so" loved us that He gave us Jesus Christ and He (Jesus) bore our sins on the cross for us. All we must do is just believe on Him. No greater love than this, than a man lays down his life for a friend. There is not a friend like Jesus Christ anywhere, he looks beyond our faults and sees our needs. When there is no one to call upon, you can always call on the Lord. He'll be there right on time. In getting my life back I now know not to put my limitations on the Lord, it will come together in time enough to give God the ultimate praise, whatever the time and however long it takes.

She suffered an intracerebral hemorrhagic stroke at age twenty-nine, and developed epilepsy from the stroke.

Lori Vober

She is a walking miracle, and felt called to share her story, and her journey of faith and perseverance, to encourage others. Lori believes God has a plan for each of us, but life is about your choices. Even with her difficulties, Lori and her husband, Dainis, were able to become adoptive parents to a sibling group of three.

She published her first book, *CHOICES: When You Are Faced with a Challenge, What Choice Will You Make?* March 2022 and has been connecting and encouraging others to choose to survive and thrive. Her book received the 2023 Reader's Choice Awards from The Christian Literary Awards in the categories of Christian Living and

Testimonial. By fall 2023, she will be a published author in four additional books as a compilation author.

Website: www.lorivober.com

Email: lorivober@gmail.com

Facebook: https://www.facebook.com/lori.vober/

Instagram: https://www.instagram.com/lorilonghorn99/

In an instant, our lives changed,
but that is where faith steps in
- Our plans aren't always the
same as God's plans

Lori Vober

Before the Stroke

I grew up in a very loving home as an only child. My dad
had a career as a businessman in the telecommunications
industry, and my mom was an early education school
teacher. With my dad's career, we moved every few years
during my childhood so by the time I had reached high
school, I had lived in several cities in Georgia, along with
the states of Alabama, North Carolina, and Texas. I spent
my high school years in the suburbs of Dallas, Texas in
a city called Bedford and absolutely loved it. Although
it was often hard to move every few years growing up,
especially as an only child, and always being the new kid
in town, those moves taught me some very important life

skills. I learned to be flexible, make new friends, jump right into new groups, and persevere when things were challenging.

Up until our move to Texas, I was into sports and played basketball. I also played in the band and marching band and football are huge in Texas. So, I traded my basketball shoes in for marching ones when we moved to Texas, and marching band became a huge part of my life for both high school and college. I played the flute in high school and the flute, piccolo, and was in the big flag core in college. I attended the University of Texas in Austin and had the wonderful opportunity to be a part of the Longhorn Marching Band all four years. Although I received a wonderful education at the university, the friendships and memories I made through the band and its sorority were priceless, and I still keep in touch with many of those same friends today. I had the opportunity to serve in leadership positions in the band's sorority and those experiences taught me so much. Through those college years, I had the opportunity to serve as the sorority's treasurer, secretary, and president. I truly believe many of my skills that I use today were established because of my experiences within the Longhorn Band and band sorority. I recently heard a DJ on a Christian radio station say you never know when a moment will turn into a memory. As I look back on my college journey, I have so many memories and experiences to be thankful for. One example that stands out is my try-out experience going into my junior year. Every summer, we have to try-out again to be part of the next season's Longhorn Band. I was already voted in as the sorority's secretary but when the results were posted, I had not made the list and was cut from the band. Thankfully, God had instilled in me the trait of perseverance, starting in my childhood! Flag core try-outs were still a few days away so my friends taught me all I needed to know and I tried out for the big flag section. I could have given up when I was first cut from the band and missed out on the Longhorn Band and my sorority for my last two years of college and into Alumni Band after graduation. Instead, I found a new love and continued in the Longhorn Band. That special trait of perseverance has served me well through the years and carried me through my stroke recovery.

I decided to follow in my dad's footsteps when it came to career choice and majored in Business and Marketing, earning a Bachelor in Business Administration degree. The summer after my sophomore year, I accepted a sales position in Austin, Texas selling ad space for a campus magazine called "Campus Concepts". It was wonderful experience in sales and cold calling, and I learned a lot. The summer after my junior year, I accepted an internship at Michelin Tire Corporation in Greenville, South Carolina. My summer job entailed market research, and this gave me the opportunity to learn a whole other side of my trade. Upon college graduation in spring 1996, many of my friends stayed in Texas, but I was very career driven and had received job offers with a petroleum company in Oklahoma, as well as, with Michelin in South Carolina. With the petroleum industry position, after I finished my training in their headquarters and received my own territory, I would manage my own convenience stores and gas stations. This position would give me the opportunity to use advertising, marketing, management, and sales skills. Because of the diversification of this position, I chose this option, which was a company named Phillips 66, and was off to Oklahoma.

I grew up attending both Methodist and Presbyterian churches as a child but because of our different moves, there was a time in junior high and high school that my family stopped going to church. Both my parents were busy working by this point, and I was on my own much of the time. Our high school was located next to a Baptist church and one of my friends, Traci, invited me to attend with her my senior year of high school. It was during this time that I finally heard the message of salvation and the idea of a personal relationship with God finally clicked. I am so glad I made that decision, accepted God as my Personal Savior, and had that foundation going into my college and young adult years. Now that I had graduated from college and was an adult living on my own, I decided church would be a good first step to finding friends. I lived in a smaller town called Bartlesville, Oklahoma and really liked it a lot. I had found a church I really liked, a good group of friends, and loved the company. The only trouble was I was antsy to grow my career, and this is where the grass always seems greener on the other side, until you get to the other side. I had been training in Bartlesville for about six months when a new opportunity opened up for me to have my own territory as a Retail Territory Supervisor. Not knowing any better, I said, "Yes, I would take the promotion," and was sent to Minnesota in January 1997. If anyone has seen the movie *New in Town* with Renée Zellweger and Harry Connick Jr., that was a great example of my new life. I was trying very hard to be a good team player but had never seen that much snow in my life, let alone try and live in it or in those frigid temperatures. When they say don't take your car through a car wash because your locks will freeze, it isn't a joke! The snow plows would come through at night and pile the snow up so high, you could barely see signs and driving was often difficult.

Once again, I decided church was the best place for me to make friends and so I visited the one church I could locate that was on the same street as one of my gas stations. My job as Retail Territory Supervisor was to manage six gas stations and convenience stores in the southern part of the Twin Cities for Phillips 66. It was a great job as it utilized so many different marketing and management skills, but the snow and weather were very difficult for me to adjust to. I made some friends at the church and one of my new girlfriends, Alana, eventually introduced me to Dainis, who is now my husband. I did not meet Dainis right away because his mom had just passed away from a sixteen-year battle with hormonal cancer. I did not understand how impactful that was at the time in my life, but God has a plan for everything. Dainis and I started casually dating, but I was quite over-whelmed with my career and the living environment. I went back to Texas in the spring to be a part of my college roommate's wedding and the last thing my parents said when I left to travel back to Minnesota was just maintain status quo. Keep working, don't make any major changes, and we will figure everything out. Well Dainis knew I was unhappy and he was worried that I might move back to Texas so while I thought we were just casually dating, he was getting quite serious. The next week, when I came back into town, we went on a date to our favorite pizza restaurant and walk around the lake in St. Paul, which was typical of many of our date nights. We were supposed to go to a couple's Bible study after our walk, but halfway around the lake, he popped the big question! After the initial shock, I said, "Yes, with a long engagement." We had met in March and it was now June 23, 1997. When I called my parents that night and told them I was engaged, I think their first question was, "To whom are you engaged to?" I am not sure at that point if I had even told them I was seriously dating anyone. Dainis was an aircraft machinist at Northwest Airlines during the time and already building a house with his cousin, who was a building contractor. In his mind, he had found true love, had a good job with a steady income, and would soon have a house, so why not move forward. He had watched his dad lose his mom and he knew life was short. We flew to Dallas the next weekend to meet my parents. Over time, I made the decision to resign from my job at Phillips 66 and started planning our wedding, which was to be held in Las Colinas, TX on March 28, 1998. I thought I was moving to Minnesota for my career, but I now know God moved me there to unite me to my Godly mate.

After we were married and settled in our house, I accepted a position in the sales and customer service side at Northwest Airlines, working with the preferred travel agency community in January 1999. I loved many aspects of the position, and my building was attached to Dainis's hanger. During those first years of marriage, we enjoyed our travel benefits and at times, Dainis even had first shift. He transitioned from machinist to mechanic and earned his Airframe and Power plant license. He also started back to school to complete his Bachelor's degree at Embry-Riddle Aeronautical University. We decided to add a dog into the mix because they always say first try parenting a dog before a child! Our first try at parenting was a cute and very energetic Border Collie named Tasha. So, it was a very busy time for us, but we were very blessed when I look back at all we were able to accomplish. We traveled to Montreal, Toronto, Cancun, Bahamas, Jamaica, Maryland, Georgia, Texas, Florida, and Norway on our flight benefits during those first few years of being married.

As we were approaching our fifth year wedding anniversary, we had been trying to start our family for over a year and had not yet been successful. We had not looked into any infertility testing at this point and just thought it may be stress related. We were on opposite work schedules, and life was very busy. I worked normal business hours and Dainis generally worked second shift, odd days off. The opportunity opened up at our church for the Office Manager position. I was already serving at our church as their special events coordinator and wedding planner, along with my job at Northwest. It was now January 2003 and if I accepted this position, it would be a big transition from my airline job. I was in a customer support role with preferred travel agents and really enjoyed helping others. However, I also had a huge desire to become a mom and struggled with using my skills for a greater purpose. My parents had moved to Minnesota to be closer to us since we were trying to start our family so the flight benefits from my airline employment were not as important to them as it was when they lived in Texas. We would still have flight benefits through Dainis's employment, and it could mean less stress and definitely less travel for me. I decided to make the career switch and normally on Fridays, I am alone at the church because the rest of the pastoral staff has that day off. On this particular Friday, three weeks into the job on January 24 th , I had a co-worker working with me in the office and a Women's Bible study was going on down the hall.

Stroke and Recovery

I started feeling sick to my stomach, had a headache, and my left arm felt a little odd mid-morning on January 24, 2003 but at age 29, I was not thinking about the signs of a stroke. It was a strange day from the beginning because we were having multiple fireplaces installed in our home, Dainis and I had a small argument about fireplace measurements just as I was walking out the door, and I broke my mirror off my car pulling out of the garage. When I started feeling bad, something told me I was not well enough to drive home so I called Dainis, who advised me to call my parents, who lived closer to the church. As I explained how I was feeling, they immediately knew something was wrong and planned to come by the church and check on me. As I was sitting in my chair at my desk, my left leg suddenly went numb, and I fell from my chair. My co-worker called 911, and we then knew something was very wrong. I saw my parents when they arrived at the church, but by the time we were in the ambulance, I was unconscious. I had suffered a massive stroke called an intracerebral hemorrhagic stroke. There are two types of strokes: ischemic and hemorrhagic strokes. Hemorrhagic strokes account for only 13% of all strokes and are the most deadly type of stroke. The paramedics rushed me to a nearby trauma center in St. Paul, and I underwent a five- hour brain surgery to stop the brain bleed. My mom was in the ambulance with me and at one point the paramedics radioed the hospital that they did not believe they would make it in time. I can't imagine the thoughts and feelings my mom experienced, and it is truly a miracle that I not only survived but continue to thrive post-stroke the way that I have. The stroke was caused by an undetected malformation of blood vessels on the right side of my brain. It was something I was born with but no one ever knew about the malformation until the blood vessels ruptured. I made it successfully through the surgery and woke up seventeen days later from a drug induced coma on life support, completely paralyzed on the left side. In an instant, our whole lives had changed. I thought I took the job at the church in order for us to start a family, but I now believe it may have saved my life. This is where once again, our plans and God's plans aren't always the same.

I remember when I first woke up from my coma, being very scared and unsure of where I was. Although the memory of those first hospital days isn't quite clear, I remember being very uncomfortable and my legs always ached from not moving. I was also quite sick to my stomach after first waking up because I was being given codeine for my pain but no one knew at the time that I was allergic to codeine, and it was making me sick to my stomach. Those beginning days were just hard days as I had to learn to do everything all over again. Swallow, eat, talk, sit up, balance and stay sitting up straight, eventually stand, and then walk with assistance. My mom stayed with me the whole time, rarely leaving my side. I had a second brain surgery on February 26th, a month after my stroke, to remove the malformation so another stroke would not occur. Although life was very hard for all of us during this time, I was blessed with several things. One, the rehab unit of the hospital was attached to the hospital so I did not have to travel far to go to the rehab floor. Many patients have to go to a completely different facility for their rehabilitation. Because I had a second surgery, I am thankful it was all at the same hospital and just a matter of transferring to different floors. In between my first surgery and second, I was in rehab and then after my second surgery, I was back in rehab. Two, the hospital was equipped with an indoor pool and part of my daily therapy was pool therapy. I believe one of the reasons I was able to start walking again as quickly as I did was because of the pool therapy. Three, I believe God really protected me emotionally through the stroke by helping me look at my recovery from a physical aspect. I always liked to work-out prior to the stroke so in my mind, if I could keep exercising and working hard enough, I could get better. Although in some ways this was not realistic, I now believe having this motivation and view point kept me going and kept me from falling into a depression or emotional spiral. My whole focus at the time was to push as hard as I could in therapy to get better. Those days in the hospital once I was on the rehab unit consisted of two occupational therapy sessions, two physical therapy sessions, and pool therapy each week day. The day would end with a shower and then dinner. I remember two of the hardest things about that time were my lack of independence to do the simplest things on my own and my lack of privacy. My family stayed with me while I was in ICU and on the general hospital floor, but I was alone once I got to the rehab floor. I remember not being able to even roll over by myself in the middle of the night and having to call a nurse to roll me over or lay there uncomfortable all night long. It was also very difficult to give up your modesty. I had to have a nurse help me to the bathroom and give me a shower every day. Sometimes being able to do the simplest of things, makes a big difference. I had caring in-patient therapists though, and I still keep in touch with them today on social media and through yearly Christmas cards.

Although I made progress, after two months, I left the hospital in a wheelchair. At that point, I could transfer and stand with help, walk very short distances with assistance, used a large plastic AFO brace to protect my ankle from turning and a quad cane, had little range of motion in my left arm, and no movement in my left hand. We went to live with my parents because our house had too many stairs, and they could then be my caregivers while Dainis was at work. Although I had been discharged from the hospital, I was still going back frequently for outpatient physical, occupational, and pool therapy. Those were hard days! I also didn't realize it until I was discharged but Dainis's career in the airlines was not going well due to the slowdown in the aviation industry from the September 11th terrorist attacks. By spring, two months after my hospital discharge, unfortunately, he was laid off. We had gone from two healthy lifestyles with two incomes to no incomes and I was completely disabled in a six-month period.

One night, Dainis went to the grocery store for us and randomly grabbed his Northwest Airlines jacket. We call this our "banana moment" but should be called "God's moment". While he was picking out some bananas, a stranger asked him if he knew a manager from Northwest. Apparently this manager used to be his neighbor, now lived in Arizona, and managed an aviation maintenance facility. Dainis did know this manager and by the end of the conversation with this stranger, he was equipped to call this manager and inquire about job opportunities. Before long, we were on our way to check out Goodyear, Arizona!

Sadly, we never did go back to our first house to live but just to pack up. There were too many stairs throughout the house and with Dainis's job situation, staying at my parent's home was the best choice. It was a difficult time of transition with a lot of good- byes and losses. We had to say good-bye to our first dog, Tasha, who we decided to leave in Minnesota. She was a Border Collie and would not be happy in the Arizona heat. Our first house was very special to Dainis because his mom helped him find the land to build it on before passing away and now we were leaving. We were saying good-bye to all of Dainis's family, our friends, our church, and our support system. In the best of circumstances, a move is hard. Looking back, this time was unbearably tough!

Once again, we thought God's plan was to bring us to Arizona for Dainis's career. However, soon after our move, we found a new neuro rehab facility for me that was perfect for my stroke recovery. So, although the move has provided good income opportunities for Dainis, I don't believe my recovery would be where it is today had we not moved to Arizona. The heat and weather has provided wonderful independence for me, and I was one of the first patients at this new clinic, called SWAN Rehab. The founder, Dr. Kay Wing, has a great passion for helping those who have suffered a stroke or other brain injuries and believed in the ability of the brain to re-learn through repetition of tasks because of the brain's neuro-plasticity. Although I had good care in Minnesota, the message was if you aren't well in six months that is all you will recover. That was not the SWAN philosophy at all. I became a patient in the fall 2003 and worked six to eight hours a day either at the clinic or at home for the next eight years to get my independence and function back. The program has changed some over time but when I first became a patient at SWAN, it was an all-day program for four weeks. We would even eat lunch and take a short nap during our time together every day! My therapy time would include walking on a machine called the Lite-Gait that was similar to a treadmill but body weight supported for safety, matt work with pulleys, strengthening exercises, and many different hand and arm activities. What I loved about Dr. Wing and her therapists were their focus and ability at changing the activities up in order for us to achieve success. Even with all my hard work, I still have a disability today but can walk independently, have better range of motion in my left arm, can use my left hand as an active assist to my right hand, can drive, and take care of our family. I have had the opportunity to work with numerous therapists at SWAN Rehab over the years, and many are still connected with me today and made a great impact on my life. They provided emotional, social, and physical support to me at a time when my whole world was turned upside down. They also introduced me to a number of products and techniques that truly made a difference in my recovery. As the program changed, my lifestyle changed, and I continued to make improvements, my intensity at SWAN changed. Although my program changed through the years, I remained a constant patient and always grateful for their help. It has now been twenty years since my stroke. After a long break, I am back in therapy several days a week, learning new things, trying new medical treatments, and continuing to make progress. Being at the clinic with your therapists is a very important part of your recovery but insurance does not pay forever. It is equally important for you to be able to have a good home exercise program and continue working hard on your own, practicing what you learned during your therapy sessions.

When I moved to Arizona, I also found an amazing physical medicine doctor that continues to monitor my medication and care today. I unfortunately experience a lot of muscle spasticity from the stroke, which is very common. It is like a continuous conversation loop from the brain to the muscles to keep firing, but it causes tightness and often makes it hard to get your body to do what you want it to do because of it. I am on a daily medication called Baclofen and get several Botox shots in my arm and hand every three months. I have learned that everyone is affected differently by their stroke and brain injury and we all have different degrees of challenges. I am grateful for the therapy, different medicine options, and new medical treatments available to help in our recovery. There is not one right path, and I continue to learn so much on this recovery journey.

One thing I think we all struggle with as a society but it becomes even more intensified when we have an unexpected challenge like a brain injury or a stroke is our anxiety and worry. We worry about all of the things we can't control and when we our lives drastically change in an instant like mine and possibly yours did, we simply have no control. That feeling of no control can easily make us slide down a tunnel of worry and anxiety and then everything just feels worse. We start worrying about how we will move forward past the stroke or brain injury, how we will recover enough to go back to work, how we can live in this new life and be happy, what happens if I never recover as much as I want, and what if no one likes the new me yet I can't change any of it. The list goes on and on of worry possibilities. Bottom line, there are things we can control and things we can't. In order to control our worry, anxiety, and be the emotional and mental healthiest we can be, we must learn to take control all of our thoughts and our attitude. This is where our faith and prayer steps in. Philippians NIV 4:6-7 reminds us, " 6 Do not be anxious about anything, but in every situation, by prayer and petition, with thanksgiving, present your requests to God. 7 And the peace of God, which transcends all understanding, will guard your hearts and your minds in Christ Jesus."

Bethany Hamilton quoted in her documentary that "It doesn't have to be easy. It just has to be possible." Dr. Wing and my therapy team at SWAN Rehab did just that for me over the years. They took what looked like an impossible situation in the fall of 2003, added their support, encouragement, and expertise, and made recovery possible for me. The journey has not been easy and although I am a very positive person, some days are still hard and frustrating. It doesn't need to be easy; I just need it to be possible. Between my faith in God and the journey He has me on, my friend and family support systems, and my therapy team, I have learned anything is possible.

Taking your
life back

In 2010, we decided we were at a crossroads. I could continue with therapy and our current lifestyle or we could look at family planning again. We had supported kids through Compassion International since we were first married and really had a heart to be parents. After moving to Arizona, my brain started interacting with the scar tissue from my surgeries and blood deposits from the hemorrhagic stroke, and I started having seizures. So along with rehab over the years, I was also faced with epilepsy and seizure management. Life was not easy at times, and the seizures were pretty scary until we got them under control. The seizures were more difficult to deal with emotionally than the stroke because there was no control. With the stroke and rehab, I felt like I had some control by working hard to get better. With the seizures, it was just a matter of finding the right medication and dosage that worked. So, because of my seizures and disability, we decided it would be best to consider adoption rather than our own biological children. Because of our years of support to our Compassion children, we were drawn to international adoption. After researching the options and based on where we lived, we chose to focus on Latino countries. Because of my medical history, Ecuador and Peru both said "no" but Colombia said "yes". We originally started our adoption journey with two boys in mind but God hand-picked a sibling group of three for us instead. Our sibling group was made up of two girls and one boy. So on April 12, 2011, we adopted a sibling group of three from Colombia, South America. Because Dainis and I had both grown up as only children, we liked the idea of a larger family. The kids were ages six, eight, and ten at the time of our adoption. Not only did we want to be parents, but we felt called to give kids a forever family that may not ever have that opportunity. James 1:27 NIV says, "[27] Religion that God our Father accepts as pure and faultless is this: to look after orphans and widows in their distress and to keep oneself from being polluted by the world." So our adoption journey began. We had fundraisers, renovated the house, purchased clothing, bedroom furniture, toys, learning manipulatives, and home-school materials. We sent the kids gifts, attended training sessions, completed all of our adoption paperwork, and went to our local community college to learn the Spanish language.

Our time in Colombia was much longer and more stressful than we originally anticipated it would be. When we decided to adopt from the country, they said plan to stay in-country for six to eight weeks. One advantage of Colombian adoptions is once you are united with your children, they stay with you throughout the entire adoption process. So, we were united on April 12th and went to stay at an adoption hotel. The first ten days is considered a grace period and then all of your paperwork is sent to a judge for final approval. Unfortunately, we got the one judge that was against adoptions and our stay in Colombia lasted almost sixteen weeks. Except for the hotel owner, none of the staff at the hotel spoke English so we truly were immersed in the Spanish language. Many situations would have been comical had we not been so stressed! There were many challenges with the kids and stressful times, but we finally flew back home on July 19 th . We did have the opportunity to meet and bond with other families that were adopting and still keep in touch with a few of them today.

Because the kids were behind educationally, did not know the English language, and my mom's background was in early childhood education, she agreed to help me homeschool the kids. So I traded in my therapy hat for mom and teacher hats. We started from the very beginning on how to hold a pencil and write on lined paper at a pre-school level. We worked very hard every day and the kids learned a lot. If we could have continued, the kids would have been in great shape educationally. In just that one year, we were able to teach them so much. Unfortunately, there were a lot of resistance and cooperation challenges. Our kids came from a world of no expectations when they came into our family. We were unprepared for so much and every challenge was a learning process along the way. Although our hearts were in the right place, it became evident after that first year we could not continue being first time parents, grandparents, and teachers and be successful. So sadly, we sent them to school the next year. Over the years, we have experienced both blessings and challenges in our parenting journey with older adopted kids. We gave our kids a better start in life and direction than they would have had within the foster care system of Colombia and supported, nurtured, guided, and loved them to the best of our abilities. We truly want them to now just live their best adult lives and be happy, successful, responsible, and independent.

When we moved to Arizona, it was very difficult at the beginning to make friends and get connected. I had just had my stroke so no one knew the real me and the first thing they saw was my disability. I think many stroke survivors and those with a brain injury struggle with this new "identity crisis". There are a lot of changes, and you have to figure out who the "new" you is on the inside and outside. For me, the struggle was more difficult because we threw in a cross-country move, and I did not have the comfort of friends that knew the "old" me to fall back on. I had to start all over with the "new" me. My therapists at SWAN Rehab were a huge support system during that time as they provided the physical, emotional, and social support I needed and desired. It took time for me to get my confidence back, to find my way, and to make new friends. The seizures also complicated this time immensely. Slowly, we got involved at a church called

Desert Springs Community Church, both in Sunday school and in the Women's Ministry. Over the past few years, I have had the blessed opportunity to lead a table of women during our weekly Bible study and currently do that both in person and with a group on ZOOM. Because connection and fellowship were difficult for me during that transition time right after my stroke, I am passionate about connecting with others now and providing that connection opportunity. I never went to formal counseling after my stroke, seizures, or to learn how to better cope with our parenting challenges but see great value in getting that formal support. Stroke and caregiver support groups have also become much more prevalent in recent years, and I definitely would have benefited from support and fellowship systems like that in those first few years of stroke recovery.

Along with figuring out what our "new identity" is and what the next step in our journey looks like after a stroke or brain injury, is getting past our physical disability and limitations. As a society, we are focused so much on outward appearances. I believe one of the biggest challenges and obstacles we face as stroke survivors is our own self- consciousness towards our physical disability. I know for me today, after working hard for twenty years, I still have a definite disability. Although it is part of my story and testimony and in certain aspects that is good to have, it is also a frustration. If we are to be truly honest, none of us want to stand out and be different but in cases such as stroke, where we are often left with a physical disability, we truly have no choice but to accept it. That is where your self-confidence and inner beauty comes in. There are things we can control and things we cannot control. I can control how hard I work at my therapy to continue to improve, my attitude, and my self-talk. I cannot control how quickly my body recovers if it does recover, what others think, or how others react to me. For our own best emotional and mental health, it is important to concentrate on the things we can control. Our attitude affects so much of our journey and who we are.

During the fall 2020 and winter 2021 when the COVID pandemic started hitting us all, I took my Bible study group on ZOOM. It was during this time that God caught my attention and I felt Him say, "I saved you from a stroke and gave you a story to share so start writing." So, I started typing out my story, joined a writer's tribe, started making connections with other writers, and then attended my first virtual writer's conference in July 2021 called "Speak Up". I had talked about writing a book in the past and had even outlined a draft but thought it originally would be all about my stroke journey, what I learned, and the equipment I used to get better. Once I started writing, the book became a story of not only the blessings and challenges we had faced over the last twenty years but the choices we made in light of our trials. I included reflection questions at the end of each chapter so it was not just my story but also an opportunity for the reader to reflect on their journey. Things quickly fell into place, and I was set to publish my first book with a hybrid publisher called Trilogy Publishing March 11th, 2022. The title of my book is *CHOICES: When You Are Faced with a Challenge, What Choice Will You Make?* One of my main messages is that life rarely turns out exactly like we pictured it would and we all face challenges along the way. When we do, we have choice of how we react to our circumstances. I quote it in my book as one of my favorite Bible verses from Jeremiah 29:11-13 NIV that says, " [11]For I know the plans I have for you," declares the LORD, "plans to prosper you and not to harm you, plans to give you hope and a future. [12]Then you will call on me and come and pray to me, and I will listen to you. [13]You will seek me and find me when you seek me with all your heart." So many times, my plans did not start out the same as God's plans but because of my faith in Him, it worked out and I could see His purpose in my journey.

In December, one of the leaders of my writer's tribe encouraged us to pick a word for 2022. I thought the word PURPOSE would be a good one given that my book was about to launch, and I would be going to my first in-person speaker training in July to perfect my skills. I based it off of Proverbs 19:21 that says, " [21] Many are the plans in a person's heart, but it is the LORD's purpose that prevails." Well, I have learned no matter what to keep my eyes on God for the bigger picture and opportunities because you never know where life will take you. Just as I was kicking off my Facebook book launch in February, I went to my doctor for a routine exam. Unfortunately, she found a cyst and after an ultrasound and blood work, she was very concerned that we were looking at a pre-diagnosis of ovarian cancer and referred me to a gyno-oncologist. This was not part of my book launch plans! However, God is so good, and we had just recently met our new next door neighbors. I remembered that my neighbor said she worked at The Cancer Treatment Centers of America (CTCA) and loved it so I reached out to her. Not only did she work there but she was one of the scrub nurses for the head gyno- oncologist at CTCA. I said no matter what the diagnosis was that I would share my story there and there had to be a reason for the timing. I was able to share my book with my doctor team and received wonderful support from the very first phone call. After my book published in March, I had a full hysterectomy and an appendectomy on April 6 th and my cyst came back benign. Thankfully, today I am cancer free. My surgeon did discover during surgery that I was missing my left ovary and tube and the right ovary was not functioning correctly. This explains our inability to conceive the year we were trying before my stroke. Because our adoption journey has been one filled with blessings, challenges, and many unknowns we were not prepared for, I have often wondered if we should have researched more the avenue of having our own biological children, even though everything pointed to no with the seizures and disability. This surgery confirmed we would never have been successful and that is just one more layer of unexpected emotional healing. This also confirmed once again that we were not only meant to be adoptive parents but God hand chose our three specifically for us. When we go through any difficult challenges, medical, life, or parenting, we often don't understand why and it is easy in the moment to question the "why". This is where our faith and God's bigger purpose and plans come in.

We often don't find the answers to our hard questions this side of heaven, but when we depend on God through our challenges, He can use those as opportunities and for a very special purpose. I know that our kids have had a better life and start here with us than they would have had they not been adopted. As parents, we all do some things right and some things wrong. Hopefully we have been an example to them of persevering through your challenges, working hard, being financially responsible, staying committed to one another through the trials, the importance of trust and relationships, and loving with your whole heart.

Once I recovered from my surgery in June, I started volunteering at CTCA, sharing my story, and connecting with others. I had the opportunity to teach about writing, journaling, and provide writing prompts so patients could consider writing as one more healing tool. I designed a four-week Bible study titled *Finding God's Purpose during Your Medical Journey* for the patients and had the opportunity to lead it at the hotel and cancer center. I did not have to go through the chemo, radiation, pain, and other treatment plans a lot of cancer patients have to endure. However, I do understand what it's like to receive a cancer diagnosis and not know what is next. I also understand from my challenges with stroke and epilepsy that with any medical journey, the road can be a lonely one. My goal is to use my story and all of the challenges and experiences I have been through to connect with and support others and bring hope and encouragement where I can. I am forever grateful God used a cancer diagnosis to give me an opportunity to start sharing my story. My time volunteering at CTCA brought new perspective, connections, and forever friendships.

One of my heart's desires is to share my story and what I have learned on my journey as both an author and a speaker. I had that opportunity on a small scale through my volunteer opportunities at CTCA, through my experiences as a Bible study leader, and through the many podcasts and interviews I have done since my book was published. I had the opportunity to participate as a speaker in two virtual conferences this year. My therapy clinic, SWAN Rehab, which was originally started in Phoenix, opened up another location closer to my home in Goodyear and they started a stroke survivor support group at this location. I had the opportunity to speak at their first meeting. God has shown me that based on my experiences, my focus group is the stroke and brain injury community and so I continue to look for avenues to support different groups within those communities. I have been given the opportunity to speak to and support several groups already, and I am thankful for every opportunity God gives me to share my story in order to help others. I attended my first in person speaker conference last summer call Christian Communicators Conference in Texas. Although it was an amazing opportunity to learn from experts, get new head shots, and walk away with a video reel for event planners, just as important was the connections and friendships I made during this special time. It is a small conference and the tribe of support and lasting friendships I have walked away with are unbelievable. The experience was unforgettable and life changing.

Just before by stroke occurred, Dainis and I were about to celebrate our fifth wedding anniversary. When I received the news of a possible cancer diagnosis, we were about to celebrate our twenty-fourth wedding anniversary together. We have travelled through tough medical, life, and parenting challenges together over the years, yet our love for each other and commitment is stronger than ever, and I have God to thank for that. I truly believe it goes back to my statement earlier that I thought I was moving to Minnesota for my career but God knew the bigger plan and what was ahead. He knew I would need a special mate by my side to withstand the stress of what we would go through and Dainis was already equipped from watching his parents' love and commitment to each other during his mom's long battle with cancer. Dainis learned by watching what it meant to take care of a wife with a medical challenge and now he was putting those skills into action. Looking at marriages today and how easily they crumble, I don't believe a lot of men would have stood by me through the medical challenges like Dainis has. Although we have our normal fights and frustrations with each other, like any normal couple, I am very grateful for his love and dedication to me. I can always count on his support and encouragement, even when he doesn't understand what I am feeling or going through. We recently had the blessed opportunity to celebrate our milestone "silver" anniversary. I look forward to walking hand in hand for the next twenty-five plus years with him. New challenges and blessings will flower our journey, but I know I can always count on his love, support, and commitment.

As the kids have now reached adulthood, and we are now entering our "empty nester" years, we have really tried to capitalize on our future, what that will look like, and what we want. Many couples put all their time and efforts into their kids and families, which is important, but once the kids leave, they are left as strangers in their home together. They let their relationship die along the way. We have been through too much for that to happen and during a vacation a few years ago, we found a vacation spot we loved. It is an area a few hours north of Phoenix called Pinetop. It reminds Dainis of Minnesota because it has beautiful trees, walking paths, and a lake, similar to the one we would go to on our date nights. We invested in some land in a gated community a few years ago, with the plan to build a retirement house one day. Because building materials are quite expensive now, we just invested in a small manufactured home as a short-term opportunity. This will allow us to vacation in Pinetop more often, become more familiar with the area and confirm that we truly do want to build a retirement home there, and if we do move forward, we will have a place to stay. Dainis is capable of doing a lot of the finishing work himself. I believe part of our ability to stay positive is to have plans and goals for the future to look forward to.

When you go through any medical crisis, but especially something as life changing as a brain injury or a stroke, therapists both in-patient and out-patient tend to have set guidelines of what they need to teach us as survivors to get back to life and function to our best abilities. I truly have been blessed by some wonderful therapists through the years and have also learned to be my own best patient advocate. Unfortunately, many times, the professionals teaching us can only understand up to a certain point because they are not living this new life we are now forced to live. They are gifted at helping us regain our mobility, independence, and needed skills but no one addresses some of the hard personal questions. How do you handle your menstrual cycle when you are a young female stroke survivor with balance issues and now only have one hand? What does sexual intimacy realistically look like with your partner after a massive stroke? How do you find your way into a "new normal" and not get stuck at the point of your stroke or brain injury? Who can I turn to when I need answers and help? These are all of the things that I believe are not always addressed in therapy but are still a real part of a survivor's world. Luckily, more stroke support groups are available today, Facebook groups, and other avenues for support. I spent most of my stroke recovery persevering in therapy to get better, regain what I had physically lost, and to fit in again among my peers. As I have matured, learned from others, and become more reflective on my journey, I realize that my lack of vulnerability and transparency hurt me in some ways. We often look at those attributes in our society as a weakness and whether we are a thirteen years old or fifty years old, we all have the same heart of just wanting to fit in and have friends. When you change your mindset though and think about your vulnerability as being an opportunity for someone to bless and help you, it changes the way you think about your situation and how you view others who may also need assistance.

I believe we all have a story, are on a journey of self-discovery, and God has given each of us a purpose. Some know their purpose at an early age and for some, it takes a lifetime to discover what that purpose is. For me, I am thankful God has shown me my purpose through my challenges. I am currently in the process of now writing my second independent book, which will be a 31-day devotional. I decided though to not only include my story and experiences in the daily devotional but to also include an excerpt from another author each day. One of the books I read was *Unstoppable* by Nick Vujicic. Nick said in his book that he finally realized there was a purpose in his challenges and he could use what had happened to him for a reason. Those statements changed my thinking, and fueled my passion and drive to use the challenges I have positively persevered through to bring hope and encouragement to others. God has taken my skill set of marketing, my passion to help and connect with others, and combined it with all my challenges to put me on this new journey. I will always be thankful God blessed me with a positive attitude, the ability to persevere, to look for opportunities in the midst of the obstacles, and to keep my faith strong and my eyes on Him for direction, even when the plans don't make sense, and find success in my "new normal" rather than getting stuck. We often don't have control over the unexpected challenges that come our way, but we do have a choice in how we react to our circumstances. I am so grateful that God showed me that writing and speaking were avenues for me to share my message and help others and so grateful He combined the whole package together.

As I move forward in my journey to help others based on my challenges and experiences, I hope to continue with my writing and speaking. My first published book, *CHOICES: When You Are Faced with a Challenge, What Choice Will You Make?* It was nominated for four categories at the Christian Literary Awards. It won 2023 Reader's Choice Award for Christian Living Day by Day category and Testimonial category. I was honored with the nominations and absolutely thrilled it won twice. I truly want others to be encouraged that even in our challenges we still can have hope, joy, and success in our "new normal". I felt like having a word and verse to concentrate on helped me, so my 2023 word is gratitude based on 1 Thessalonians 5:16-18 NIV that says, "[16]Rejoice always, [17]pray continually, [18]give thanks in all circumstances; for this is God's will for you in Christ Jesus." It is a choice we have to make every day and although it is not always easy, it is possible to find joy even during your difficult challenges.

Romans 8:28 NIV says," [28]And we know that in all things God works for the good of those who love him, who have been called according to his purpose." We all have a purpose in this world. When the picture doesn't turn out like we planned or even wanted it to, I believe we just have to keep looking for the purpose in what we are going through, what we can do with it, and how we can use it to help someone else. After being on this journey and learning all that I continue to learn, one of my future goals is to start a podcast for stroke and brain injury survivors so they have a home to tell their story. *Everybody Has a Story, and Every Story Has a Purpose.*

One of my favorite children's fables is The *Tortoise and The Hare.* Although you can grasp different lessons from this important story, in light of our disabilities, I am reminded that we are all on our own journey. As hard as it is to not compare, it is important to remain true to yourself and the purpose you have been called to live, and remember in the story who won the race. Like the tortoise, those of us who have suffered a brain injury or stroke may be slower physically or mentally but slow and steady, taking one measured step at a time, wins the race. We can't change our past but our tomorrow is full of possibilities with the right perspective, mindset, attitude, and perseverance.

After suffering a stroke in 2017, jewelry-making helped her to regain her dexterity while in rehabilitation.

Michelle Herndon McKay

53-year-old, Michelle Herndon McKay was born in Michigan and is married with a 19-year-old daughter. She was raised in Arizona from the age of four. Crafts have played a part in her life and are a part of her family's history. After suffering a stroke in 2017, jewelry-making helped her to regain her dexterity while in rehabilitation. She can look at something and know how to incorporate it into a craft. She has always been creative; crafts and writing - she has a love for words also. The most recent stroke has intensified those talents and she cannot wait to be in full creative mode again. She uses her experiences to give back, and help other survivors, especially those who have suffered strokes.

Before My Strokes

I was born in Trenton Michigan, an only child to adoring parents. We lived close to family for the first four years of my life. But due to my health issues, I got pneumonia a lot, we moved to Phoenix, Arizona, and warmer weather. My father was a civil engineer and my mother worked different jobs that allowed her to put her family first. We lived so far from relatives that we became the family version of the Three Musketeers. My parents took me everywhere they went and taught me to be well-behaved and polite. I was Daddy's girl in angel wings and my Mama's sweetie pie. I was spoiled to a point and grew up in the same house from the time I was seven years of age until I was engaged to be married.

I grew up dreaming of being a wife, and mother. I had fabulous expectations of a white picket fence, a loving husband, and staying at home with my children. I wanted the fairytale but soon found out that they don't exist. I found out very quickly that I had led a very sheltered life.

I discovered that the things that seemed wild to me, were very normal in society. I had grown up a naïve, chubby kid so I was a good friend to most guys, but never the girlfriend. I was very creative, enjoying drama, art, and writing poetry in my youth. I also started attending church with some of my friends, but those friendships faded after graduation. After high school, I skipped college because I just wanted to get married and have children. I was determined to make my dream a reality.

After high school, I started working full-time in a depart-ment store. I oversaw the Woman's Plus size department. I lived at home, paid rent, and enjoyed new friendships at work. My life consisted of working, sleeping, and going dancing whenever possible, I was a happy camper. I had found friends and activities that gave me joy. One night while out dancing I met my first serious boyfriend and future ex-husband. He was in college, tall, good-look-ing, and interested in me! This was a first for me and of course, I thought of all the possibilities. We dated exclu-sively and became serious quickly. He even taught me how to drive and helped me get my driver's license which opened a whole new world for me. After 18 months of dating, he proposed, and I accepted. We were engaged thru his senior year of college, and we lived together while planning our wedding. He had witnessed a very messy divorce between his parents, which was quite trau-matic for him. The normal stresses of wedding planning and living together were added to by my fiancé's fear of a failed marriage. We both had our own visions for the future which were very similar but not the same. The wedding went as planned; all I had dreamed of. Being a Daddy's girl had guaranteed that it would be the wedding of my dreams. We had a beautiful honeymoon in Mexico, then returned home to settle into married life. Matt worked for his father as a computer specialist. I stayed home and took care of the house and him, in my mind that was my job. I was 19 years old and living my dream! Before our 6-month anniversary, Matt received a job offer from The National Security Agency. We were off to live in Maryland, and while he worked as a tech specialist, I was the happy homemaker. All was great, except for missing our friends and family. I missed my parents so much. Meeting and making friends was more difficult than expected. The marriage went downhill fast. My parents came out for our 1-year anniversary and brought the top tier of our wedding cake to us. After they left things got worse. Matt left for work two months later and flew home to Phoenix. His father called me to tell me that Matt was leaving me. Feeling abandoned and alone, I tried to take my life. Luckily a friend came to visit me and called 911. I left the hospital and flew home to my parents two weeks later. Matt shipped my belongings to me and I picked up the pieces of my life in the safety of my parents' home. I made new friends, took some college classes, and worked two part time jobs. I was determined to have the life I had always dreamed of and not to let myself be broken. I became stronger and more determined to be the woman I was meant to be. So I started to build my wall of unfulfilled expectations to protect myself. Little did I realize that wall would eventually become my prison.

After returning home, I went job hunting. Eventually landing two retail positions. Both part- time, both in retail. I worked at Lotions and Potions and a record store. Then my mom convinced me to check out Beauty School. Which I enrolled in and loved. I was on my way to rebuilding my life. An opportunity to build the life I wanted. I joined a church and started attending activities with the Singles Ministry. I also made new friends to hang out with. Every Saturday night we attended a church dance where I learned all the country line dances, the two-step, and the west coast swing. It was one of my favorite activities and it allowed me to meet like-minded singles. It didn't take long for me to start dating some other church members, but none of them ended in a love connection.

I got a new job, one full-time job in a salon as a receptionist. It was the perfect job for someone attending beauty school. Hair became my passion and I excelled at it. I put my romantic dreams on the back burner and threw myself into work and school. I still went to the church dances with my friends. But didn't really date, until one of my friends introduced me to a guy she had met. His name was Buck, and we had so much in common. After about a month of dating, we went to church and attended all the dances together. We were a couple, and everyone knew it. Every day, he brought me a single red rose to remind me how special I was to him. He would bring the rose either to my school or work. Other times he would leave it on the windshield of my car. It was amazing and we were engaged after six months. One day we were walking around the mall and Buck pulled me into a jewelry store to look at rings. Two weeks later he proposed at the church dance in the parking lot. My feet didn't touch the ground all night. I was floating on air and in love.

Our engagement lasted a couple of weeks until one Friday night, we decided to elope. We called my parents and asked them to go with us. We all took off on Saturday morning for Las Vegas. We stopped for breakfast and then drove to The Little White Wedding Chapel. We wore our best Western clothes and boots. It was cool; in my mind, he couldn't wait to marry me, but in reality, he was getting tired of being on his best behavior. After getting married I finished beauty school and took my state exam to get my cosmetology license. I passed my test and earned my license. I was ready to start doing hair in the salon. Everything was great. Things were falling into place; I was married, a hairdresser, and ready to start a family.

Unfortunately, Buck had other ideas, totally different ideas. Six months into the marriage he became very controlling and abusive. I fell in love with one man and ended up married to a very different man. I had no idea what to do. I couldn't make a move without his permission and if I did, he became very angry. We attended church on Sunday and Buck made sure that my bruises were always hidden under my clothes. I was too embarrassed to tell anyone. We went to counseling which only made Buck more abusive. I even had a cat that would attack Buck when he abused me. The abuse went on for six months and I couldn't figure out what I was doing wrong.

My Mom saw the bruises one day when we were shopping and started asking questions. Once we got home, I broke into tears and told her everything. After my confession, she called some ladies in our church group, and I was packed and moved into a studio apartment before the end of the day. I was safe and had my cat, but once again single and childless. Buck hadn't wanted children till our "ducks were in a row". So, with another failed marriage, I built my protective wall a little higher.

This was the first time I had ever lived alone. Everything was the way I liked it. It was full of my tastes and preferences, and I loved it! Cowboy the cat seemed quite happy also. We had so much in common, he was the purrfect roommate. He didn't hog the bed or covers, and he wasn't a picky eater. He also never left the toilet seat up. This is when my great love and appreciation for cats began. Cowboy loved me just the way I was. He loved me unconditionally and was always ready for a good snuggle. Life was good, but I still had my dreams which were going to happen, I was more determined than ever. We lived in roommate bliss for a few months. I worked, shopped, and ran my own life for once. I was pleasantly surprised by my competence. Cowboy spent his days lounging around and taking cat naps on the windowsill. Two peas in our own little studio apartment pod.

After my divorce was final, I decided to get back out there and mingle. I started going to the singles meeting at church. Which led to new single girlfriends and new church dances and singles activities. We met new guys and dated new guys and just enjoyed being single. I found comfort in the fact that I had God in my life to guide and support me. It always seemed to be a problem that I was divorced when I met someone at church. I decided to just be social outside of church activities. Some of my friends decided the same thing. So, we started to widen our search for our soul mates. Hopeful romantics on the hunt. I met guys thru friends and hoped to make my dreams a reality. I met lots of sweethearts but not the ones. Finally, one of my work friends from the salon was introduced to a friend of her husband's. Cody and her husband worked together at a sporting goods store. Cody was a big snuggly teddy bear. I did hair and he sold guns at work. Then outside of work, we fell hard and fast for each other. In six months, we were ready to tie the knot. We planned a beautiful wedding and reception to be held in my church and went on our honeymoon to visit his family. We married in October and honeymooned over Halloween. The wedding almost didn't happen, while I was in the bride's room with my grandma, mom, and bridal party, I got cold feet, but my grandma reminded me that I was lucky that someone was willing to marry me after two divorces. After that reality check I took a deep breath and got married like a good girl.

After the honeymoon we came home and transferred to a one-bedroom apartment in my current complex. It was close to both of our jobs and friends. We settled into married life, and I learned things about my husband that shocked me. I already knew he had no car and no belongings besides guns and clothes. But then I found out that he had never filed a tax return, never made a payment on his student loans, and was incredibly irresponsible. What was going on? I was completely freaked out and scared that the IRS was going to make me homeless because of my husband's carefree lifestyle. Right then and there I became a control freak to protect the life I had overcome obstacles to attain.

I knew our marriage was over, the first time he hit me. I had no intention of going through that again. I immediately pulled back and added more bricks to my wall to protect myself. Cody tried very hard to get past what he had done with flowers and surprises. But I was over it and ready to be single again. I would take being single over being a punching bag. Cody swore he would never hit me again, but I wasn't willing to find out. I had been through that journey before and didn't wish to go again. So, six months into our marriage Cody moved out and filed for divorce. As the song goes "Another One Bites the Dust!"

After Cody, it was just Cowboy and I again. We slipped into our comfortable lifestyle. My Daddy retired and then my parents sold their home and moved back east to be closer to my Mom's side of the family. That had always been the plan, so it came as no surprise when it happened. Cowboy and I had each other and I was perfectly happy with the situation. I gave up on getting married and dated as a fun distraction from the everyday. I worked, went to church, and enjoyed my life. I of course had a couple of long-term boyfriends because you always find what you aren't looking for. But this time Cowboy helped me decide on second dates. When my date and I would sit on my loveseat the cat would jump up for pets. If the guy gave Cowboy attention, then he got a second date. If the guy ignored Cowboy, then he got the claws, and I never went out with them again. It was like Cowboy was part of the package, almost like I was a single Mom. All in all, Cowboy was a pretty good judge of character most times. A couple of guys slipped under the radar.

The most memorable guy that got through the Cowboy test was Ed. I met Ed at work when I gave him a haircut. Even though I tended to screw up my personal life, I excelled at work. I climbed the management ladder effortlessly. My area supervisor became my mentor and friend. Ed was seven years older than me, charming and handsome. He knew what to say and when to say it. I really liked Ed and I was pretty sure he liked me. We were together for two years, and after six months I told him that I loved him, and he replied "Ditto!" He introduced me to his family including his grandmother. They were all very kind and I looked forward to being related to them. Ed talked about getting married and he always told me how special I was. He spoiled me rotten and made sure I knew he cared, be he never said, "I love you." Those words were very important to me. So important that I gave him an ultimatum, on our second New Year's

Eve together. I told him that he needed to tell me "I love you" by midnight either by words, a card, or a letter. If he didn't, we would be over. We spent the holiday with his parents and when the clock chimed midnight he spoke not a word, therefore I ended us, and started the New Year single. It broke my heart, but I stayed strong, and Ed didn't try to get me back. It was horrible, I beat myself up trying to figure out what was wrong with me.

I hibernated with Cowboy for a while. Only going out for work, church, and great sales. It didn't make my friends very happy, but it was what I needed to do. Only time can truly heal a broken heart, and I was ready to be over Ed. After a month my girlfriends were upset with me and decided to force me to get back on the dating horse. Some of them took me dancing, and Maggie talked me into signing up for a radio dating service with her. I basically did it to get her off my back never thinking I would meet anyone. But meet someone I did, someone very special. His name was Bill, and he was a Transportation Specialist, which translates to a truck driver.

He left a message for me on the dating service, and I left him a message on his answering machine and never heard a reply from him. I went on a few interesting first dates to keep my friends happy, and I stayed true to my Cowboy. Then one evening I checked my dating service messages and got a message from Bill. His message basically told me I shouldn't be on a dating service if I didn't return messages. This really made me angry, so I called his home number once again and left a mean message at 3 a. m., figuring there was no way he would answer, and I could get my message left. Much to my surprise, he answered! So, I told him that I had called him a couple of weeks earlier and he realized that he had written my number down incorrectly. He had been leaving messages on the wrong voicemail for two weeks. That was why I hadn't called him back, after we figured out that great mystery with him yelling at me, I hung up on him figuring it was over, but he promptly called me back. This kept up for about ten minutes, he would call trying to convince me to go out with him and I would hang up on him. I finally agreed so he would stop calling me. I agreed to go to a Drive-In movie with him after work the next day. Keep in mind that it was 3:30 in the morning. Bill called me that evening at work to get my address and to figure out which movie we would see.

Bill showed up early that night in a ratty t-shirt and torn jeans, needing a haircut. Being a hairdresser, I had taken the time to look good, and he had not. I was not impressed by him, but his truck was gorgeous. A 1996 royal blue, Dodge Ram, extended cab, 4x4, perfect for a Drive- In movie. I had brought pillows and blankets to make the truck bed comfortable for movie viewing, still holding out hope that the date could be salvaged. Unfortunately, Bill was very forward and expected the date to go a different direction than I did. The date was disappointing for both of us. But that night I dreamed about going four-wheeling with Bill in his truck. So, the next morning I called him and told him about my dream. I proposed that we should only be friends and that I would love to go up north with him. I even offered to pay for gas and supplies. He agreed and picked me up in 30 minutes, no make-up and a ponytail in comfy clothes we took off for a day of fun.

Bill was a totally different person that day. He was polite, funny, and kept his hands to himself. I had a great time, and by the time he brought me home, we were holding hands. It was time for him to meet my roommate, Cowboy. So, I invited him in and offered him a drink. We sat on my loveseat talking for a while until Cowboy decided to join us. I hoped they got along because I really liked him. Cowboy jumped up for pets and Bill took the hint. He scratched all the right places and Cowboy purred his approval. Jackpot! Knowing that Bill would be gone for the next week for work, I made sure that he knew I had a great time. He assured me that he didn't want a serious relationship and proved he was an amazing kisser before he left. We talked every night for the next week while he was on the road. During our last conversation that week he asked me to be his girlfriend. I told him that I had rules for putting the final bricks on my wall. I truly couldn't handle another broken heart, but the romantic in me was hopeful. Bill was handsome, fun, and a great kisser. I thanked God for another opportunity for love.

Bill's job as a long-haul truck driver kept him on the road for three weeks at a time, then home for three days. It worked out well, for three weeks I could tend to my world and work without complications. Then the days that he was in town I set aside everything but work. It was all about us and I gave my attention to him. We talked every night for a couple of hours which helped us to get to know each other very well. While I still had the safety of my walls around me, my apartment walls, and my personal wall of unfulfilled expectations. When he was in town and I wasn't working, we were together. If he was with his parents or friends, I was with him. His mom became my other Mother, and his parents were my family when he was on the road. They had me over for dinners and I did my laundry at their house on my day off. I even had a key to their home and sometimes left surprises for Bill in his room for when he got home. Once again, I was in love and looked forward to the future. Ironically, we talked about marriage often but not married each other. We used statements like "When I get married…" never using the word we. It was a safety net for both of us. Then on our first Christmas in front of his family, he gave me a promise ring and proposed! It was unexpected and amazing! His sister and mom were just as excited as I was. Three months later on my birthday, we went out to dinner with his family, and he surprised me with a rose and my engagement ring. The ring was tied into the bow on the rose. We took our time picking a wedding date, working around my work commitments, and hunting season. We agreed on March 17, 2000, for our day. I am very Irish and always loved that day, it worked around all our limitations and was a Friday that year. The salon which I managed now would be fine without me and it wouldn't interfere with hunting season.

We started planning quickly, I would find things that

we discussed while he was on the road, and then when he came home, he would check things out. Bill was the only man that I had ever met that wanted to help plan his wedding. His mom and I would look for things while Bill was working. I even had my wedding dress made by a seamstress from three different dress patterns. Our wedding was a Western-themed affair. Outdoor at a ranch, we were married on a hay wagon. Bill and our dads wore Western side arms and Stetson hats. No tuxedos, no bridesmaid gown. An outdoor wedding with a buffet dinner and dancing under the stars to a DJ. My parents and grandma came to town for the wedding. My Dad walked me down the aisle but first asked me if I was sure. I assured him that I was, and I got married. Everyone seemed to enjoy the wedding, it was definitely a good mix of both of us. Bill surprised me with a wedding night reservation at a local hotel. My parents went back to our apartment and Bill took me to our hotel. We honeymooned in San Diego by ourselves, not visiting family or friends. We stayed in a hotel and started our marriage journey just the two of us.

We started our family much sooner than we planned. I was six months pregnant on our one-year anniversary. The pregnancy was a joyous surprise, but nonetheless a surprise. Bill changed jobs to an in-town position to be home with his family. I became a working mom, sometimes working more than one job, but I also strived to give my family the perfect life of my dreams. I was determined to out-do even June Cleaver. My life changed so much, I went from taking care of a cat and myself to taking care of a child and a husband. I held myself to such a high standard with unreal expectations and pushed myself constantly. I even stayed up while they slept to gain extra time to meet my personal goals. I became a control freak and perfectionist trying to hold my family to unrealistic expectations. I would get upset when things were not done my way not realizing that at least it was getting done.

Everything came crashing down one night when exhaustion overtook me, and I fell asleep while driving home from doing inventory. Bill and Caitlyn had come to the salon to be with me, and Caitlyn had wanted to ride home with me. I was driving northbound and traveled across a main street to be awakened by my car hitting a lamp pole. The police called Bill and Caitlyn and I were taken to the ER by ambulance. This made me aware that I was doing too much and that things needed to change. I left doing hair and became an administrative assistant. Which gave me a more suitable work schedule for a working mom. My nights and weekends were spent with my family.

Our marriage had its ups and downs just like any marriage, but we survived it all because we decided that divorce was never an option for us. My husband was amazing and loved me thru my craziness. He was a great father to Caitlyn and adored her. I worried more about being a friend, while Bill fell into his parent role easily. I worried more about being fair and spoiling our daughter, I set boundaries for her in the kindest way I could. Bill was a stricter parent than I was, and it worked well.

Caitlyn was the first and only grandchild in the family, my parents watched her while Bill and I worked. Bill worked a night shift for AAA, and I worked days. We had found our routine, working, spending time together as a family whenever possible, and doing laundry and errands on Saturday, then off to church on Sunday. This was how life was supposed to be. Caitlyn had regular phone calls and visits from Bill's parents. Our daughter knew she was loved, and she thrived. I always made her my priority, making sure I was available for school events and PTA meetings.

As she got older, she would sometimes tell me that I was around too much, more than other moms. I was determined to be a hands-on momma no matter what and when I got stuck at work, then my parents stepped in and attended events. Caitlyn became very close to her grandpa, and my dad, and watching them together was delightful. When my parents moved into a new home, one room became her room with a bunk bed, toys, dress-up clothes, and games. She even had a trampoline and wading pool at their house. It was her home away from home. My Mama used to say that watching Caitlyn reminded her of when I was little. Holidays started out at their house but eventually moved to our house when we rented a larger home. This of course caused me to put more pressure on myself, everyone's happiness was my responsibility. I had very unrealistic expectations of myself, perfection was my only option. Nothing less would do for my family. The stress of trying to be perfect and control everyone's life eventually caused health problems. It was at this point that my personal wall of protection came tumbling down. It had taken years to build and seconds to destroy, but health issues will do that.

My Strokes

After achieving my dream of becoming a wife and mother, I stressed myself into Type 2 Diabetes and dangerously high blood pressure. These two conditions and my lack of self-care eventually led me to my first mini-stroke at the age of 49 in 2017. I had this stroke while making photocopies at work at the end of the day. I got dizzy and had to hold myself up with the copier. I drove myself home and went to bed early because I had a weird tingling sensation on my right side. I went to work as normal in the morning, still feeling odd. My coworker noticed something wasn't right and insisted that I call my doctor after I told her what had happened. I had to leave a message with his medical assistant. Within minutes I received a call advising me to go to the ER immediately. I let my boss know that I needed to leave, then called Bill who met me at home and took me to the hospital from there. I had an MRI which confirmed that I had suffered a mini- stroke.

Testing revealed that my blood sugars and blood pressure were out of control, therefore I was admitted to the hospital.

While in the hospital I had a second mini-stroke, which added intensity to my deficits. I had challenges but pushed through them and worked from my hospital room with my laptop and cell phone. While in the hospital I had trouble getting eating utensils to my mouth. One day my parents came to visit me for lunch and my dad helped me learn to feed myself again. It is one of my last memories of him and an example of his constant love and support for me. He was and always will be my hero. I got a lot of my strength and determination from him. I stayed in the hospital for a week and then returned to work when my blood sugar and high blood pressure were under control.

On my first day back at work I fell asleep at my desk. My strokes had affected me more than I had realized. My employer insisted that I work part-time until I finished my outpatient therapies and was feeling better. Testing in Physical and Occupational therapy revealed all the challenges I had acquired. I went to outpatient therapy three days a week for several months. I returned to working full time and everything seemed to be back to my pre-stroke skills. Then over a weekend in 2018, I suffered a third mini-stroke which compromised my vision. It was about 1 am on a Saturday morning, I was on Facebook and suddenly I lost sight. Within about 15 minutes my sight returned but I had double vision. Bill had woken up when I yelled his name, and he took me to the ER. I was given an MRI which revealed a mini-stroke with a small brain stem bleed. They sent me home Sunday morning and recommended I follow up with an eye doctor and my primary care doctor as soon as possible. When I had my follow-up appointment, I was informed that I should have been admitted to the hospital for further testing and treatment.

At this point, I left my job, added vision therapy, and enrolled in a vocational rehabilitation program at Rehab Without Walls in Phoenix, Arizona. It was an outpatient clinic that I attended daily for about six hours a day. I received all types of therapy, speech, occupational, physical, cognitive, and psychological. All these therapies were to help me return to work. After completing the program, I returned to working part-time at a resale shop that was owned by a family with a daughter who had a brain injury. It was a great job that understood my challenges, I loved working there. I joined a social group for Brain Injury Survivors, and I was moving forward in my recovery journey. The resale store went out of business shortly before COVID hit the states. I went to work as a customer service representative at a call center and ended up working from home in 2020.

On the morning of June 22, 2020, my alarm went off to wake me up for work. When I opened my eyes, the room was spinning and I was dizzy and nauseous. I realized something was wrong and I called Bill who was already at work. I told him something was wrong, and that I needed help. After hanging up I attempted to stand up but could not. Sitting up just caused me to become dizzier and start vomiting. Bill called Caitlyn who was still asleep and then called his mother who rushed over to our house. I have an amazing mother-in-law, Donna who is always there for her family, I call her my other mother. They both came into my bedroom to see what was wrong. After determining my symptoms, they called my primary care doctor who advised them to call 911 which they did. At this point, I don't truly remember much, and my daughter Caitlyn will be telling the rest of what happened during this time.

"I remember getting a call from my dad the morning of which my mom had her fourth stroke and brain bleed. He called me around 7:30 in the morning saying "Mom is throwing up and feeling extremely dizzy, go help her however you can. I'm going to call Gramma and have her come over too". After receiving this call, I got up and went to my mom's room thinking she just had the stomach flu, and boy was I wrong. When I got in there, she was throwing up everywhere and was extremely delirious, wasn't making sense of what she was saying and to be honest it scared me because I didn't know what was going on. I was trying to get my mom to aim for the trash can so she wouldn't throw up on herself more while my grandmother came and called her doctor. During this point, I was trying to get my mom to be more stable and nothing was working. My grandmother came in and said we need to call 911, with me knowing more about her medical history I was the one to call 911 and my grandmother took over trying to take care of my mom. When I called, I gave them all of the information and they transferred me over to emergency medical and they came. When they did their initial overview of my mom, they said that she seemed okay and that she probably just had the stomach flu which I knew wasn't right. I told them everything about her medical history and made them take her to the hospital in an ambulance. When they loaded her up, I tried to get in the ambulance with her and was told I couldn't because of COVID. This broke my heart and caused me to worry more because I didn't know what was wrong with her. About an hour later my dad came home and we called the hospital to see if there were any updates and unfortunately, we only received the answer, "She's in the middle of testing, we'll call you back when we have more information". This only caused my father and I to worry more. A couple of hours later we got a call from the hospital but not from a nurse, a social worker, or even a general doctor, we got a call from a surgeon.

They said that my mom had another stroke that caused a brain bleed and that she needed emergency surgery to have a drain be place into her brain to release the fluid and the pressure from the bleed, if not this could kill her. My father consented to the surgery because my mother was in and out and was unable to. Once the doctor hung up the phone, I remember my father and I breaking down because we were unable to see her and we didn't know what the outcome of this surgery would be. Amid waiting, panicking and praying I contacted her workplace to tell them what was going on and we weren't sure of when the outcome would be. Afterwards I called every family member we have and told them what was going on with my mom, asked for prayers and tried to take care of not only myself but my father too. A few hours later we received another call saying that my mom was out of surgery, and she was going to be okay, but she was placed in a medically induced coma so then the drain wouldn't be bothered and she would be able to rest. After this my father and I continuously called almost every three hours to get an update on her, to the point where the nurses started knowing our voices. A few days later my mom was out of the coma but was still in and out. When the nurses told me this the first thing, I did was FaceTime my mom because we couldn't see her. One of her amazing nurses answered the call and held the phone up to my mom and I held back so many tears because I could finally see my mom. When I saw her, she was still delirious, she wasn't making sense when she spoke, and she had a half-shaved head with a drain popping out of it. I had so many mixed emotions, I was happy that she was okay, I was sad that I wasn't able to be there to hug her and hold her hand and I was worried about her because I couldn't take care of her myself. After this we kept calling and getting more updates and I remember the day where my mom was coherent enough that she was able to call us by herself and it was the most joy filled moment we had in two weeks."

I woke up in the ICU around 3 a.m. and my first question was if I had COVID. Then I asked to call my husband, and the nurse told me what time it was, but I insisted to call him anyway. He answered and didn't seem to mind what time it was. After hearing his voice, I fell back asleep since I was still very weak. I was being fed and medicated by a tube with a drainage tube in my brain. It was a while before I was tube free. At that point, I was put in a room and watched closely. I talked to family daily, but no one was allowed to visit me in the hospital due to COVID. I was surrounded by amazing medical professionals, but I felt so alone without my family. I was in the stroke unit at St. Joseph's Hospital with excellent care, the nurses and aids were super sweet and kind. As I got stronger, I started working with in-patient therapies. My family brought me clean clothes regularly and picked up my dirty clothes also. I was not allowed to see them, but they stayed in touch with my nurses and brought me whatever I needed.

I started being scheduled for physical therapy, occupational therapy, and speech therapy. I had a lot to work on, things that I knew I had to do, but my body didn't quite know how to do right then. My blood pressure and blood sugars were a big concern for my doctors and monitored them closely. All I could think about was getting home to my family. I threw everything into my recovery, I started off dragging my feet with an upright walker. Eventually with being able to walk with a regular walker, but still need a wheelchair for longer distances. I had a vision and dexterity challenges also, but my balance was my worse challenge to overcome. I took my recovery very seriously and was determined to get home. I threw my all into recovering. I coped with not seeing my family with phone calls and Hallmark movies. At one point, my physical therapist told me that I might go home in a wheelchair. I told him that if he did his job correctly, I would walk into my home and I did. I spent seven weeks in the hospital. The doctors wanted to transfer me to a care facility before sending me home, but my family vetoed that idea and took me home.

Recovery

Once home, my mother-in-law, Donna, became my daytime caregiver, and my husband and daughter took over at night. They got me thru the deepest depression I have ever known. During this time, Caitlyn kept my employer updated, and Donna got my long-term disability set up. This was a very difficult time. I prayed for death daily and scared the heck out of my family. They loved and supported me, and we got thru it. I will be forever grateful for the family I have been blessed with. They played a huge role in my recovery. It is true that a stroke happens to the entire family, not just the survivor.

Our family pets also played a part in my recovery. From the moment I came home, either one or more of them was by my side. It didn't matter if I was asleep in bed or resting in my recliner, they watched over me like furry angels from above. Our smallest dog Charlie was the most attentive and protective of me. He was stuck to me like glue from the time my husband went to work until the time Bill came home. He didn't care if I was home alone or not, he was taking care of me. Two of our cats, Cheddar and Romeo were also quite aware of my need for extra attention. Both spent lots of time keeping me comfortable and distracted. Their requests for attention kept me busy many times when I was feeling lost and alone. I believe that animals know when we are ill or in distress and they will do their best to give us aid. Our pets are a blessing sent to us from above to help us on life's journey.

Armed with some knowledge from my previous strokes, I threw myself into recovery. I was determined to get my life back. I attended outpatient therapy several days a week, working with the same OT and PT that I had worked with years before. This helped because we knew each other and worked well together. Insurance eventually decided that I had done enough therapy, as they often do. What I eventually found out was that my old life was no longer an option. Things would be different. I contacted the state and applied to get back into the Vocational program again. I was quickly scheduled for an evaluation with a Neuropsychiatric. It was determined that mentally I qualified for the program. It was during this appointment that my overactive creativity kicked in. During my lunch break this day I wrote the following poem:

"The Woman Looking Back at Me"

I look out the window and what did I see?
I encountered a woman looking back at me.
She had short brown hair and hazel-colored eyes,
She appeared to be me to my surprise!
She had no walker and gazed with both her eyes.
I wanted her to speak but she uttered not a word,
I was being a little bit absurd.
Reflections do not speak.
As I reflected upon whom I have become,
I saw none of my challenges in the reflection that I saw.
She looked quite normal,
Nothing out of the ordinary.
But, looks can be deceiving.
People can see my walker,
And lacking sense of balance.
They can hear my slurred speech,
And see my missing dexterity.
At first glance she could be my twin,
But when people look closely the similarities will end.
We will be the same someday.
After hard work and therapies,
*My goal is to be more like **THE WOMAN LOOKING BACK AT ME.***

I was scheduled for another evaluation at an Outpatient rehabilitation clinic called Rehab without Walls. This evaluation was more physical, and it was determined that I was not ready for the program yet. I received this news on my 53 rd birthday. They gave me a balloon, wished me Happy Birthday, and said that I wasn't ready yet.

That setback only motivated me to work harder. I started vision therapy and volunteered with BIAAZ (Brain Injury Alliance of Arizona). During this time, I realized that my survival was a calling from God to inspire and motivate other stroke and brain injury survivors to live their best life. I wanted to help them understand that their life wasn't over, it was just different, and different can be joyous! I wanted to return to work but I wanted this to be my job. I came up with the concept of Marvelous Motivations. My creativity was in overdrive at home making crafts and motivational cards. I was still going to vision therapy which was rather expensive and not covered by insurance. Donna made sure I attended all my therapies and doctor appointments which helped because I couldn't drive due to my vision.

My primary care doctor decided to send me for more outpatient therapies eventually and I was referred to Swan Rehabilitation Center. Again I was evaluated to find out what I needed to work on and what my goals were. I expressed a desire to return to work part-time and found out that they also did the vocational rehab program thru the state. I was recommended for the program and made daily phone calls requesting a spot in the program. Swan's program director was also on top of it and between the two of us, I got in! I was ecstatic and motivated; this was the beginning. I had an amazing team, my family at home, and my Swan team. I got a five-person team, Sarah/Program Coordinator, Kaitlyn/OT, Kimberly/PT, Molly/ Social Worker, and Pat/Speech therapist. I was going to succeed with this team's support.

They listened to me, challenged me, and guided me with tough love sometimes. They also kept my family aware of what was going on. I was with these wonderful people for almost 2 years. During this time I moved my vision therapy to Swan, I made some new friends and got to know the new me. I overcame my inner control freak and perfectionist. I learned about self-care, boundaries, and my value. I embraced the new me, and really liked her.

I got many opportunities to test out my new reality. While still volunteering in various ways whenever possible, I cohosted a stroke survivor event, blog interviews, and various crafts with BIAAZ. I started a Facebook group for Stroke and Brain Injury Survivors named Thriving and Surviving. I also got to do a weekly craft class at an assisted living program for dementia patients. I loved what I was doing, and I felt successful in my recovery! I had even gotten to meet Miss America. I learned how to use Dial a Ride and was able to take care of myself during the day. I was gaining more independence and I loved it. This independence made my husband and daughter nervous, but they let me grow under their watchful eye. I also always have a family member when I go to a medical appointment. Usually, either Bill or Donna will accompany me. I became successful at keeping track of my schedule, arranging rides, and attending therapies.

I was able to attend Caitlyn's college graduation, which she did amid all my medical chaos. She was a student, working girl, and girlfriend, and took care of our household. She took over cooking and cleaning and grocery shopping just to name a few things which allowed me to concentrate on my recovery. I am so proud of the woman she has become and appreciate all her love and support on this journey. My husband/Bill took over our finances while being supportive of my crafting and adaptive changes that I needed. He has bought endless craft supplies and installed various assistive equipment to help me be successful. He has also supported our family thru all of this as the only breadwinner. I was eventually approved for SSDI which replaced long-term disability but is still less than my paychecks used to be. When I came home from the hospital, I was convinced that he was going to leave me. I thought that he deserved so much more than me. I even told him this several times but thru it all he has shown me love and support in so many ways. He has helped me shower, helped me dress, done my hair, and cut my meat for me just to name a few things. This man is my rock and is always there for me.

I continued with Vocational Rehab, creating a new resume, and researching jobs in my new career of choice. I have not yet been able to control my diabetes and blood pressure constantly, so I have taken a step back from returning to work. I am using this time to incorporate more self- care into my life. I will attend outpatient therapies. I am exploring and embracing different resources available to me. This is being done to achieve a better life balance. I am working on being imperfectly perfect and giving myself grace. I am hoping to find opportunities to inspire and motivate others, which is why I am telling my story. I hope that my journey will show others that stoke survival is a gift. An opportunity to reinvent yourself and enjoy your life. Don't be afraid to ask for help or search out resources available to you. Embrace your new community of survivors and know that you are more than enough and trust in God's plan for you. I honestly got my life back the minute I awoke from my coma, at that point I was alive. Then over the last three years, I have found my best life. I know that my recovery will be a lifelong journey. I am excited about my future and overcoming any challenges that I encounter along the way.

In closing, there is one more thing I would like to share. While at Swan I was asked to write a 'Thank you letter' to my stroke. At the time I thought it was crazy but later found it to be therapeutic and it put things in perspective. I hope it will inspire you to write one.

Dear Stroke,

I wanted to take this opportunity to "Thank you" for all the positive changes that you brought into my life. First impressions can be deceiving, and I was not impressed by you when we first met. But since you have taken me on this journey. I have come to learn so much about myself and what is important to me.

Below I have listed some specifics for you…

- Thank you for the opportunity to stop working, and for allowing me more time for this process.
- Thank you for not killing me but showing me how precious life is.
- Thank you for giving me such intense creativity, which helped me to stay active and allowed me to help others with crafting activities.
- Thank you for making me a better writer and poet. It is such a joy for me.
- Thank you for making me need to embrace my BI community and search out my community

resources.

- Thank you for teaching me that self-care is so important and that my family is very capable of taking care of things. Plus, it is ok to ask for help.
- Thank you for showing me how amazing my family is.
- Thank you for showing me, my passion for helping others.
- Thank you for helping me to create and embrace a Facebook group for stroke & brain injury survivors.
- Thank you for all the great new friends and people that I have met on this journey.
- Thank you for leaving me the ability to walk with assistance, and the ability to speak and do so much more.
- Most of all thank you for creating the necessity to reinvent a happier and healthier me. With less intensity, better communication skills, and the ability to set and respect boundaries.
- I have to say that as hard as it has been, I am very grateful for all the opportunities and lessons that you brought into my life. You actually saved my life. Instead of my life being over, it is just different.

Thank You Again,

Michelle Herndon McKay

www.ingramcontent.com/pod-product-compliance
Lightning Source LLC
Chambersburg PA
CBHW051523120626
46551CB00012B/1046